superherbs

super

herbs

herbs for health and healing **michael van straten**

mitchell beazley

Dedication

This book is dedicated to the memory of my late mother, Kate, and her sisters Ada, Minnie, Leah, Sally and Gertie, who were all wonderful cooks. Each had her own speciality, and whether it was fish, meat, poultry, soups or my mother's wonderful strudel, cakes and biscuits, they introduced me to the miracle of culinary herbs. During my student days, there were many frantic phone calls to Mum or one or other of the aunts for help with some tasteless recipe ('Add garlic.' 'It needs more parsley.' 'Did you forget the bay leaves?' 'Of course you can't cook fish without dill.' 'Potato salad always has chives…').
The advice was unfailingly right.
MvS

Superherbs

by Michael van Straten and
Sally Pearce

Superherbs is meant to be used as a general reference and recipe book. While the authors believe the information and recipes it contains are beneficial to health, the book is in no way intended to replace medical advice. You are therefore urged to consult your health-care professional about specific medical complaints and the use of healing herbs and foods in the treatment thereof.

First published in Great Britain in 2000 by Mitchell Beazley, an imprint of Octopus Publishing Group Limited, 2–4 Heron Quays, London E14 4JP.
Reprinted 2000
© Octopus Publishing Group Limited 2000
Text © Michael van Straten 2000

ISBN 1 84000 261 1

A CIP catalogue record for this book is available from the British Library.

Commission Editor: Margaret Little
Art Director: Rita Wuthrich
Executive Art Editor: Tracy Killick
Design: Miranda Harvey
Project Editor: Jamie Ambrose
Production: Karen Farquhar and Jessame Emms
Index: Ann Barrett
Photographer: Edward Allwright

Typeset in Helvetica Neue Condensed
Printed and bound by Toppan Printing Company in China

contents

introduction

Two thousand years ago, the Greek physician Hippocrates, the father of modern medicine, advised his patients to let food be their medicine and medicine be their food, and that is the purpose of this book. *Superherbs* is a combination of ancient wisdom, modern science and the alchemy of the kitchen. With it, you can produce delicious dishes that burst with flavour and overflow with health-giving nutrients, yet still serve as medicine for all that ails you.

This, then, is the true 'kitchen medicine' that has evolved, along with man himself, through time, trial and error. As we enter the third millennium, it is an appropriate time to take stock of all that has happened to the way we eat. The relentless march of the food industry, the tide of takeaways, the overwhelming presence of supermarkets and multi-billion-pound advertising budgets for convenience foods have all produced greater changes in the food we eat during the past 50 years than in the previous 50,000.

Yet does this 'instant-food' culture really matter? In terms of the nation's health, nothing matters so much. The epidemic of diseases of civilisation has been fuelled by these changes. Four and a half million men and 5.5 million women in the UK are clinically obese; if nothing changes, there will be 15 million obese British adults by the year 2010. Heart disease, high blood pressure, strokes, diabetes, arthritis and some types of cancer are all related to obesity.

Yet *Superherbs* is not a slimming, diet or weight-loss book; diets don't work. What does is making permanent changes to everyday eating habits, and that's where kitchen medicine comes in. Kitchen medicine means a greater understanding of food and its healing properties. It means putting enjoyment and pleasure back into the process of shopping, cooking and eating fabulous food. It means using Nature's abundance of fragrant and healing herbs to their best advantage.

Throughout history, the great physicians, philosophers and writers have extolled the virtues of herbs and good food as part of man's heritage. An anonymous proverb asks, 'Why should a man die who has sage in his garden?' The Bible's Book of Ecclesiastes states: 'The Lord hath created medicines out of the earth and he that is wise will not abhor them.' From *Romeo and Juliet* to Rudyard Kipling, the knowledge of herbs' power and healing properties has been pointed out time and again.

Similarly, our grandmothers may not always have understood the medicinal value of culinary herbs, but they knew how to incorporate them into everyday cooking, making soothing teas, reviving soups, protective hotpots, and energizing desserts. In that same tradition, *Superherbs* will guide you back into the kitchen with its simple recipes. Here, you'll learn how to grow, harvest, store, freeze, dry and use these wonderful plants. You'll find recipes for soups, starters, meat, fish and egg dishes, snacks, puddings, drinks, herbal teas (with, of course, vegetarian choices). There are recipes for lotions, potions, gargles, face creams and hair tonics.

The collective wisdom of thousands of years of human history and kitchen medicine is represented in this book. To use it, all you have to do is turn the page.

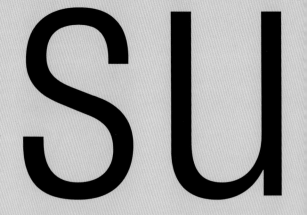

his

tory of
herbs

herbs past and

The use of healing plants or herbs is as old as the history of man himself. Traces of healing remedies have been found in the graves of Neanderthal man, in the tomb of Tutankhamun and in the burial chambers of the ancient Chinese emperors. Yet it was the Persians in 2000BC, the ancient Greeks and Romans, and the English of the Middle Ages who inspired the great tradition of what could be called 'kitchen medicine'.

In the first century, for example, Dioscorides produced the oldest of Western herbal manuscripts: *De Materia Medica*, a treatise on the use of herbs as food and medicine. Much later, in 1597, John Gerrard's *The British Herbal* became as much a gardening and cookery book as a medical reference manual. Since those distant days, herbs used for both flavour and therapy have remained commonplace. The only difference today is that we have largely forgotten the enormous medicinal value of parsley, sage, rosemary, thyme, mint and all the other aromatics we add so nonchalantly to our daily cooking.

Modern medicine, with its vast armoury of high-tech pharmaceuticals, has origins stretching back five millennia. Even now, a quarter of doctors' prescriptions are for medicines that still have their bases in traditional herbs. Digitalis, derived from foxglove, is still used to treat heart disease; morphine, taken from the opium poppy, remains the most powerful of painkillers.

Even at the sharpest cutting edge of 21st-century medicine, herbs have a vital part to play. In recent years, new recruits have joined the ranks of the tried and tested

present

plant medicines. Vincristine, for example, from the Madagascan periwinkle, has revolutionized the treatment of childhood leukaemia; taxol, from the Pacific yew, is now highly sought after as a cancer treatment. Plants have provided new drugs for everything from Parkinson's disease to high blood pressure, and many more.

So why not write a strictly medicinal book about herbs? Well, herbs are both food *and* medicine. Their healing powers and nutritional values combine quite naturally in delicious, healing and health-promoting dishes. What better way to 'take your medicine', then, than in food – its most enjoyable form? From the earliest cave-dwellers who scattered aromatic leaves on their cooking fires to ancient Romans who added wild thyme to their bubbling cauldrons or Chinese mandarins who grew healing garlic in their gardens, whole populations have understood the healing and flavouring values of herbs. This knowledge used to be passed from generation to generation, but modern man has lost the meaning behind that tradition.

It is no coincidence that we combine mint with roast lamb, sage with pork, bay leaves with rich stews and tarragon with chicken; not only do these herbs add uniquely to the flavour of the dishes, they also help in the digestion of the foods themselves. The 'kitchen medicine' of our forebears is, if anything, even more relevant to life in the 21st century than it was in bygone days. By using the knowledge of the past, we can avoid, prevent and even reverse some of the degenerative diseases of modern Western civilization.

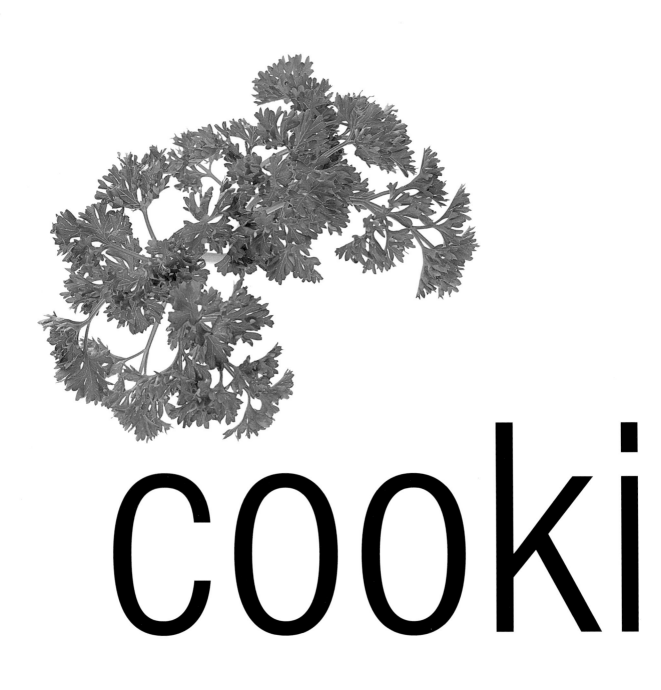

cooki

ng with
herbs

protective

Long before man discovered sulphur drugs and antibiotics, he was forced to rely on nature for protection against infection. Individuals have stronger or weaker immune systems depending on their genetic inheritance, hygiene, nutrition and emotional status, but the real miracle of evolution has been man's ability to identify and use plants which are protective.

Proof of this extraordinary knowledge is found not only in ancient texts such as the Old Testament and the *Koran*, Buddhist and Ayurvedic writings and Egyptian hieroglyphics, but also in the oral traditions of American Indians, aborigines and rain forest peoples. Ancient tombs have also been found to contain evidence of these powerful and protective plants. Fortunately, today they are not just the property of kings and emperors; you can incorporate them into your everyday life simply by using the delicious recipes listed in this section.

Modern science now provides proof that many 'herbal remedies' work, proof strong enough to convince the most hardened sceptics that herbs impart far more than just flavour. Garlic, for instance, is now 'officially' accepted as one of the greatest of all protective herbs. It is a powerful antifungal which can be used both for prevention and treatment of unpleasant conditions such as athlete's foot, ringworm and thrush. It has specific antibacterial properties and is known to kill off the bugs which most commonly cause chest infections.

herbs

Yet the most exciting area of research has proved beyond all doubt that garlic's main function is as a protector of the heart and circulatory system. It lowers cholesterol, reduces blood pressure and significantly lessens the stickiness of blood – which means that heart attacks, strokes and thrombosis are much less likely to trouble those who eat it with abandon.

In this section, you will find other common herbs such as thyme, sage and oregano, known for their antiseptic, antibiotic and antifungal properties. You will also be introduced to a host of less well-known and surprising plants, all of which will help boost your natural immunity. Some of their flavours may seem unusual, and the combinations of foods possibly even bizarre, but – personal taste and preference excepted – the recipes are all delicious and good for you. Besides, getting your dinner guests to guess the ingredients of some of them will make a great party game!

Marshmallow and myrtle, lavender and lovage, pinks and primroses all have a part to play as protective herbs. Whether it is to 'dose' children off to school for the first time, boost your resistance before surgery, recover after illness, stay well and active to meet the demands of modern living, or enjoy a long and healthy retirement, nothing is more important than making the most of your own natural immunity. Make these recipes a regular part of your normal diet, and use them especially during times of excessive stress, and you will reap the benefits of the most health-giving and nutritional foods – enhanced, of course, with some of the most protective herbs around.

The ultimate in heart protection, this soup benefits from the blood pressure- and cholesterol-lowering properties of garlic as well as its ability to reduce the risk of blood clots that can lead to thrombosis and strokes. It also includes heart-protective mono-unsaturated fats and vitamin E derived from olive oil and almonds and the super antioxidants found in black grapes.

This is the classic white garlic soup of southern Spain. Sadly, few holiday-makers try it because of the British obsession with 'garlic breath'. Don't be afraid: serve this chilled delight on a warm summer's evening – just don't tell anyone what's in it until afterwards. It is specifically heart-protective, but it's great for chest infections, too.

heart's desire

white bread 6 medium slices, stale, without crusts

almonds 175 g (6 oz), blanched and skinned

garlic 4 cloves, peeled

cider vinegar 4 tablespoons

olive oil 85 ml (3 fl oz), extra virgin

black grapes 20, for garnish

1 Soak the bread in cold water until soft.

2 Whizz almonds and garlic together in a food processor or blender.

3 Squeeze bread slices to drain excess water, then add them to the processor with a little water and whizz again.

4 With the processor still running, add the vinegar, oil and la little more water, if necessary.

5 Pour into a bowl. Add enough water to give the soup the consistency of single cream.

6 Chill. Serve with grapes floating on top.

vital statistics

Protein, fibre and protective antioxidants are the major ingredients in this delicious soup. The volatile oils in mint aid digestion of the peas and prevent flatulence. Tarragon is also a digestive stimulant and helps balance menstrual irregularities. The benefit of adding chives comes from their appetite-stimulating properties; they also function as another digestive aid.

growing tip

Chives and tarragon are expensive to buy in supermarkets. Both grow easily in pots, but they need lots of water, and chives require an occasional dose of tomato fertilizer. Allow some of the chives to flower as they are attractive to look at and delicious in salads or floating on soups such as this one.

This is a quick, easy, inexpensive and highly protective soup; what's more, the freshness of mint, the smooth touch of tarragon and the onion-y chives give a flavourful twist to an old favourite. It's perfect for anyone with digestive problems or women with pre-menstrual or menstrual disorders, and makes an ideal immune-booster for children and the elderly.

minty pea soup

peas	750 g (1 lb, 10 oz), frozen
fresh mint	2 tablespoons
tarragon	2 tablespoons
vegetable stock	225 ml (8 fl oz)
fromage frais	150 ml (5 fl oz), low fat
chives	1 tablespoon, finely chopped, plus extra (whole) for garnish

1 Cover peas with boiling water and cook, with the mint, according to the instructions on the packet.

2 Drain; add the tarragon and stock, then purée until smooth.

3 Return to heat and stir in fromage frais and chopped chives.

4 Serve garnished with sprigs of mint and whole chives.

vital statistics

Packed with protective isoflavones present in the beans. These natural phyto-oestrogens protect against breast cancer, osteoporosis and the uncomfortable symptoms of the menopause. The carvacrol in savory reduces the beans' flatulent effects, and the antibacterial essential oils in thyme add extra protective power.

This instant, inexpensive meal is as full of health benefits as it is of good hearty flavour. All beans are bursting with nutrients, but the combination of broad (or fava) beans and kidney beans contains more than most. Generally speaking, fresh is always best, but canned beans are more delicious than other preserved vegetables; just rinse them thoroughly to remove the salt.

savory fava salad

broad (fava) beans	approximately 500 g (1 lb) fresh (shelled and cooked) or canned
kidney beans	1 x 400 g (14 oz) can
spring onions	4, finely chopped
tomatoes	3, coarsely chopped
cucumber	1, peeled and diced
herb vinaigrette	approximately 150 ml (5 fl oz) of flavour of choice; *see* page 95
savory and thyme	1 tablespoon combined, chopped

1 Rinse canned beans in running water.

2 Combine all ingredients in a large bowl and mix well.

3 Cover and leave for 30 minutes to allow the flavours to blend together.

4 Serve with crusty wholemeal bread.

vital statistics

Contains **protein** from the egg, **probiotic** bacteria from the yoghurt, essential fatty acids from the anchovies, and lots of calcium, iodine and vitamin D. Sinigrin, from horseradish, protects mucous membranes; the enzyme myrosin, with powerful antibacterial properties, is just one benefit of nasturtium flowers. Capers stimulate the appetite, improve absorption of nutrients and are gently laxative.

The smooth yoghurt, the soft, delicate eggs, the crush of capers and the unexpected bite of the horseradish make this an intriguing starter as well as a good boost to the immune system. The attractive nasturtium flowers and dark strips of anchovy aren't just for decoration, either; they contribute to this dish's complex flavours as well as to its therapeutic benefits.

protective egg shell

eggs	8, hard-boiled, shelled and halved lengthways
horseradish	1 teaspoon fresh, grated (or preserved); alternatively, use 2 teaspoons ready-made sauce
capers	12
natural yoghurt	1 large carton, live, low-fat
anchovies	1 small tin, drained, soaked in milk for 10 minutes and patted dry
nasturtium flowers	1 handful

1 Place the eggs, cut side down, on a large oval serving dish.

2 Mix the horseradish and capers with yoghurt and pour over eggs.

3 Decorate with anchovies.

4 Scatter over with nasturtium flowers, serve and enjoy!

vital statistics

Low in saturated fat, yet rich in healthy mono-unsaturated fats and vitamin E, this dish provides heart, lung and skin protection, some good fibre, plenty of calcium and B vitamins. Oregano is a powerful antibacterial, and the linalool in basil relieves acne.

This colourful, tasty Mediterranean treat is a feast for all the senses. The green and red of basil and tomato set against the creamy, white cheese make it inviting to the eye, while the pungent, unmistakable odour of oregano and the delicate scent of basil create an explosion of aromas and flavours.

mediterranean rarebit

wholemeal baguette	one, cut into 2.5 cm (1 inch) slices
garlic	two cloves, halved
avocado	1 small
parsley	1 small bunch, finely chopped
tomatoes	3 or 4, sliced thinly enough to cover each slice of bread
goats cheese	sliced, as for tomatoes
basil	as many leaves as you have slices of bread
oregano	about 2 teaspoons, dried

1 Toast bread slices gently on both sides. Rub one side with the cut section of a clove of garlic.

2 Mash the avocado with the parsley and spread thinly on the bread.

3 Top with tomato slices, then goats cheese.

4 Sprinkle with oregano.

5 Grill for about five minutes, or until cheese starts to run. Add basil leaves to each slice and grill for one minute only.

vital statistics

Contains essential fatty acids, protein and minerals (especially iodine) with lots of B vitamins from the salmon. Tomatoes and red peppers supply plenty of beta-carotene and lots of vitamin C, a strong antioxidant cocktail. Chervil, tarragon and chives provide antibacteria and antiviral volatile oils. Chervil adds extra protection through its ability to lower blood pressure, and it contains useful amounts of iron.

growing tip

Sadly, chervil, which was traditionally eaten on Maundy Thursday, is one of the most ignored culinary herbs; like so many others brought to us by the Romans it has fallen out of favour. Yet it grows well in a large pot – just don't put it in full sun. A hardy annual, it will soon reach a height of around 60 cm (2 ft) and a spread of 30 cm (1 ft). Enjoy its delicate aniseed flavour in salads as well as with fish and poultry dishes.

Chervil, tarragon and chives are three of the strongest protective herbs around, and this simple dish contains them all. It also has real visual appeal, which makes for a great starter or, in more substantial quantities, a perfect light lunch or supper.

salmon maundy

herb vinaigrette	4 tablespoons; *see* page 95
basmati rice	250 g (8 oz), cooked and cold
chives	3 tablespoons, finely snipped
tarragon	1 tablespoon leaves, coarsely chopped
chervil	2 tablespoons, coarsely chopped
salmon fillet	250 g (8 oz), poached and cold
tomatoes	2 large, roughly chopped
red pepper	1 large, deseeded and thinly sliced
black pepper	freshly ground, to taste

1 Mix the herb vinaigrette and most of the herbs together; pour over rice.

2 Flake the salmon, discarding any skin, and stir into the rice along with the chopped tomato and red pepper.

3 Add a generous grind of black pepper and stir again.

4 Sprinkle over with remaining herbs.

No, the title isn't a typing mistake; it's a neat description of this delicious pasta and salami salad. The food police forbid such wonderful Mediterranean meats, but in spite of consuming them in vast quantities, our Continental neighbours suffer far less heart disease than we do. That's the result of eating huge amounts of heart-protective foods, including the herbs that give this recipe flavour.

pastami salad

pasta 250 g (8 oz) any small variety

cucumber 1, cut into julienne strips

salami 125 g (4 oz) piece, skinned and diced

tomatoes 250 g (8 oz) peeled, deseeded and chopped

herb vinaigrette 4 tablespoons, made with balsamic vinegar; *see* page 95

iceberg lettuce 1, roughly torn

fresh marjoram 1 tablespoon, chopped

welsh onions 2 stems, finely snipped

1 Cook pasta according to directions; drain and cool.

2 Mix together with cucumber, salami and tomatoes.

3 Pour vinaigrette over the mixture and chill well, turning at least once.

4 Just before serving, stir in lettuce and sprinkle with marjoram and Welsh onions.

vital statistics

Rich in heart-protective omega-3 fatty acids from anchovies, mono-unsaturated fat from olive oil and garlic, with the added bonus of vitamin C from lemon juice, tomatoes and parsley. Lemon balm has strong antiviral properties and is specifically protective against the cold-sore virus. It also helps over-active thyroid conditions.

Lemon balm (its Latin name is *Melissa*) is a remarkable herb, traditionally used as a heart-relaxer and aid to wound healing. Its volatile oils, flavonoids and tannins also help fight depression, stress and indigestion. Looking at the rest of the ingredients, you might think this recipe can't possibly work, but it does – deliciously. It's one of my favourite quick mid-week suppers.

pasta melissa

anchovy fillets 2 x 50 g (2 oz) cans

garlic 2 cloves, chopped

lemon juice of 1

olive oil 4 tablespoons, extra virgin

spaghetti 400 g (14 oz)

lemon balm 3 tablespoons, chopped

tomatoes 3 medium, coarsely chopped

parsley 2 tablespoons, chopped

1 Put anchovy fillets, with some oil still clinging to them, in a mortar and crush with a pestle until they break down.

2 Add the garlic and keep crushing.

3 Remove to a medium-sized bowl, add lemon juice and mix well.

4 Slowly drizzle in the olive oil and mix well.

5 Cook the pasta according to instructions. Drain well.

6 Stir in the anchovy and oil mixture.

7 Add lemon balm and mix again.

8 Serve sprinkled with tomato pieces and parsley.

growing tip

Always have a large pot of marigolds growing on your terrace, balcony or window-sill. Save and dry the petals (*see* page 104); not only are they great in food, you can also use them to make marigold oil (*see* page 93) and infusions, a wonderful treatment for skin problems.

vital statistics

Egg noodles provide carbohydrates and some protein. Combined with the antioxidants, carotenoids and vitamin C from the garlic and peppers, this becomes an instant protector of the heart and immune system. This recipe has the added bonus of the antibacterial and antifungal properties of marigold, the anti-inflammatory oils in coriander and the digestive benefits of tarragon.

Everyone knows how good it is to wake up in summer with the sun streaming through the windows. This recipe imparts that warm feeling, whatever the weather. Sunny, orange marigold petals combined with the fresh green of tarragon and coriander give an added lease of life to noodles.

summer noodles

egg noodles 250 g (8 oz)

rapeseed oil 2 tablespoons

garlic 2 cloves, chopped

yellow pepper 1 large, deseeded and sliced very thinly

lemon zest and juice of ½

coriander 1 tablespoon, chopped

tarragon 1 tablespoon, chopped

marigold petals 1 tablespoon

garlic oil 1 tablespoon

(*see* pages 93–4)

1 Cook the noodles according to the instructions on the packet.

2 Heat the rapeseed oil in a large wok or frying pan. Add the garlic and yellow pepper and stir-fry for one minute.

3 Add the noodles and stir-fry for three minutes.

4 Stir in the lemon juice, zest and herbs and continue stir-frying for one minute.

5 Add garlic oil and mix in thoroughly – and serve.

vital statistics

An ideal combination of protein, starch and vitamins. The phyto-oestrogens and calcium in tofu protect against breast cancer, osteoporosis and menstrual problems. The gingeroles in ginger protect the circulatory system and ward off chilblains. Nettles are an excellent source of iron, and their vitamin C content ensures it is well absorbed.

Most gardeners spend their lives trying to eradicate stinging nettles; please don't! Leave a corner where they can flourish (bees and butterflies love them) so you can enjoy their flavour and medicinal value. Here, they help make this delicious dish massively protective, as well as a complete meal for vegetarians.

stinging nettle stir-fry

rapeseed oil	1 tablespoon
garlic	2 large cloves, smashed
ginger	1 cm (½ in), grated
basmati rice	250 g (8 oz), cooked
red pepper	1 small, deseeded and diced
green pepper	1 small, deseeded and diced
carrot	1 large, grated
tofu	125 g (4 oz), cubed
welsh onion	1 tablespoon, snipped
nettle leaves	2 tablespoons, chopped
spring onion	2, very thinly sliced lengthways

1 In a wok or deep frying pan, heat the rapeseed oil and add the garlic and ginger, stirring vigorously for one minute.

2 Add the rice. Stir-fry for two minutes to coat with oil, then add the peppers.

3 Finally, add the tofu, carrot, nettles and Welsh onions and continue cooking, stirring continuously, for another couple of minutes.

4 Serve garnished with the slivers of spring onion.

chef's tip

When harvesting nettles, wear gardening gloves to gather only the pale young stems. Remove leaves (rubber gloves are essential) and use to make this – and many other – unusual recipes.

You won't find fresh bergamot or myrtle in anything but the most specialized shops – so grow your own. Bergamot, a hardy perennial with attractive flowers, grows well in a large pot. Myrtle, a half-hardy evergreen, can be planted directly into the soil against a south-facing wall, or in a pot. With your own plant, you'll be able to harvest the spicy berries, too.

This low-fat, high-protein fish is an excellent source of minerals, especially iodine. Low-fat and cholesterol-free, this is a heart- and circulatory-protective meal. Bergamot contains heart-protective and cancer preventing essential oils, especially limonene and linalyl, which aid digestion and relaxation. Myrtle leaves are generally tonic and antiseptic, and protect the urinary system from infection.

The distinctive flavour of bergamot is most commonly associated with Earl Grey tea and it combines brilliantly with fish, particularly the blander varieties. In combination with the exotic spiciness of myrtle leaves, this recipe is equally suitable for hake, cod and white tuna – the perfect dish to set before a king, let alone an earl.

earl's fish

olive oil	2 tablespoons, extra virgin
unsalted butter	60 g (2 oz)
swordfish	4 steaks
bergamot	1 tablespoon chopped leaves
rosé wine	1 glass
myrtle	8 leaves, whole
black pepper	freshly ground, to taste

1 In a large frying pan, heat oil and butter.

2 Fry fish with the bergamot leaves for around 12 minutes, turning once, until just crisp on each side.

3 Remove steaks with a slotted fish slice, leaving the juices in the pan.

4 Turn up the heat. Add the wine, then the myrtle leaves, and boil briskly for one minute.

5 Pour sauce over fish and serve.

vital statistics

Another meal rich in protein and full of B vitamins and the minerals you'd expect from deep-water sea fish. The particular protective value of capers comes from their content of capric acid. This substance increases the flow of gastric juices, which stimulates appetite and makes digestion more efficient, ensuring that all the protective nutrients in the fish are better absorbed.

As an island nation, we consume remarkably little fish compared to the amount eaten 50 years ago – and John Dory is probably near the bottom of the league table. I've never understood why. Since being introduced to this extremely ugly but perfectly textured and wonderfully flavoured fish by my neighbourhood fishmonger, it has become a firm favourite.

caperbility fish

John Dory	4 fillets
butter	4 generous knobs
dill	4 sprigs
dry white wine	1½ glasses
capers	1 tablespoon, rinsed
black pepper	freshly ground, to taste

1 Wash the fish and place on a large sheet of foil in an ovenproof dish.

2 Put a knob of butter and a sprig of dill on each fillet.

3 Pour over with the wine.

4 Scatter capers over the fish.

5 Season generously with black pepper.

6 Pull foil over fish and secure firmly at top and sides.

7 Bake in a preheated oven at 180°C (350°F/gas mark 4) for 20 minutes.

Enormous immune-boosting properties come from the mixture of six herbs and six vegetables, which give this recipe a genuine double whammy. Antioxidants, cancer-protective phytochemicals, heart-protective and antibacterial herbs combine to provide super protection. In addition, lovage is anti-microbial, while bay helps fat digestion and marjoram offers antiviral properties.

This recipe for beef is a genuine one-pot meal, as everything you need cooks together in a fragrant, mouthwatering blend of aromas and flavours. Lovage, with its unusual taste, combines well with the more traditional flavours of bay leaf and marjoram to make this dish as protective as it is delicious.

double six stew

1 Toss the cubed meat in flour, and brown in the olive oil and garlic in a large casserole dish.

2 Add the vegetables and stir briskly for two minutes.

3 Add the Guinness, the bouquet garni and water, if necessary, to cover.

4 Bring to the boil. Cover and simmer for two-and-a-half to three hours, adding more water if necessary.

5 Stir in the lovage leaves just before serving, and enjoy with some good chunky wholemeal bread.

chef's tip

To make your own fresh bouquet garni, tie together
one bay leaf with a sprig each of marjoram, parsley and thyme.
The flavours will be better than any you could buy in the shops.

lean stewing steak · 500 g (approximately 1 lb), cubed

plain flour · 4 tablespoons, seasoned to taste

garlic · 2 cloves, chopped

olive oil · 3 tablespoons, extra virgin

onion, celery, carrots, broad beans, swede, parsnip · 500 g (approximately 1 lb) combined weight, chopped and peeled as necessary

guinness · 300 ml (10 fl oz)

bouquet garni · 1 (*see* chef's tip, above)

lovage leaves · 1 tablespoon, chopped

vital statistics

The combination of the sulphurous allicin from garlic and the powerful antiseptic thymol from thyme (it's in the pink mouthwash you get at the dentist) offset the slightly higher animal-fat content in the beef. Super-rich in protein, beta-carotene and extra heart protection from lycopene, this dish is also an excellent source of easily-absorbed iron.

While the avoidance of red meat may be of benefit to those suffering from specific illnesses – high blood pressure, gout, raised cholesterol levels or heart disease – modest amounts of best-quality organic lean beef make a valuable contribution to the diet. The typical Gallic flavour of this casserole is redolent of holidays in France; just inhaling its aroma is sure to lift the spirits.

beef gaulloise

garlic 2 cloves, chopped

olive oil 30 ml (1 fl oz), extra virgin

lean chuck steak 750 g (approximately 1½ lbs), cubed

chopped tomatoes 1 x 400 g (14 oz) can

pitted black olives 75 g (3 oz)

red pepper 1 small, deseeded and thinly sliced

thyme 1 sprig fresh or 1 teaspoon dried

red wine a glass or two, to taste

1 In an ovenproof casserole, sauté the garlic gently in the olive oil.

2 Add the meat and fry until brown all over.

3 Add the remaining ingredients, including sauce from the tomatoes and enough red wine to cover.

4 Cover the casserole and transfer to a preheated oven.

5 Cook for about two hours at 150°C (300°F/gas mark 2).

vital statistics

True peppermint (*Mentha piperita*), is rich in essential oils, especially menthol and menthone. It also contains cancer-fighting limonene and is a valuable source of carotenes. As well as protecting the digestive system, peppermint is a powerful antiviral. The unusual addition of hyssop – rich in many volatile oils, especially hyssopine, and the expectorant marubiine – makes this recipe good protection against coughs, colds and the flu.

Adding mint to lamb stems from the days when most sheep were eaten as mutton, and meat was higher in fat than modern cuts. Though the digestive benefits of mint are as important as its flavour, few people think of its medicinal qualities. The unique taste of this recipe also depends on the sage, parsley, lemon juice and spices – which naturally give it even greater nutritional value.

posh hyssop hotpot

rapeseed or peanut oil	2 tablespoons	**1** Heat the oil in a large ovenproof casserole and fry meat, sealing it all over.
rag end of lamb	1 kg (2 to 3 lbs), cut into serving pieces	**2** Add the onions and fry gently for two minutes.
onion	1 large, thinly sliced	**3** Add the remaining ingredients.
vegetable stock	400 ml (14 fl oz); a low-salt cube will do	**4** Transfer to a preheated oven and cook at 180°C (350°F/gas mark 4) for two hours.
bouquet garni	a bunch of parsley, mint and hyssop tied together	
lemon	juice of 1	
fresh ginger root	1 teaspoon, grated	
nutmeg and ground cloves	1 generous pinch of each	

growing tip

You won't find hyssop in your supermarket, but it's great to grow yourself. It does well in a pot, but needs space since it grows to about three feet by three feet. Because it's covered in blue flowers throughout the summer and has a wonderful fragrance, it also makes a beautiful addition to any garden.

growing tip
It's wonderful to have a juniper tree in your garden, but take care
which plant you choose. This hardy perennial comes in a number of
varieties that range from ground-covering bushes no more than a foot high
to trees of 25 feet or so. Consult an authoritative garden manual or
ask at the garden centre before you buy. All varieties produce berries.

A chicken casserole with a difference. The combined flavours of hyssop oil, bay leaves and juniper meld with the gin, creating a uniquely tantalising taste and fragrance which permeate both the chicken and vegetables. Serve with plenty of chunky country bread to mop up the wonderful juices.

boozy chicken juniper

1 Mix one tablespoon of oil with the garlic, half the onion, juniper berries and pepper and rub into the chicken skin and cavity. Leave covered in the fridge for at least an hour.

2 Heat the remaining oil and brown the chicken all over in a large, heavy-bottomed casserole dish.

3 Remove the chicken. Add the vegetables and sweat over a low heat for five minutes, stirring occasionally.

4 Replace the chicken and add the gin, wine, stock and bay leaves.

5 Cook at 180°C (350°F/gas mark 4) for one hour, or until juices run clear.

6 Serve the carved chicken in soup plates, together with the vegetables and juices.

vital statistics

Part of the health secret of Mediterranean people is the inclusion of garlic, olive oil and alcohol in their food, all three of which are in this recipe. Protein, iron, folic acid, B vitamins, with the protective substances in onions, garlic and leeks are only the beginning. The anti-inflammatory properties of hyssop are present in the oil and enhanced by the even stronger antiseptics and anti-inflammatories pinene, limonene and thujone in juniper. Bay leaves, too, play an important role as they contain the volatile oils cineole and linalool, which improve digestion and protect against joint pain.

hyssop oil	(*see* pages 93–4) 2 tablespoons
garlic	3 cloves, chopped
onion	2 large, chopped
juniper berries	2 teaspoons, crushed
black pepper	freshly ground, to taste
chicken	1.3 kg (approximately 3 lbs)
carrot	1, diced
leeks	2, sliced
baby turnips	3, sliced
celery	1 stick, with leaves, chopped
gin	75 ml (2.5 fl oz)
white wine	125 ml (4 fl oz)
chicken stock	300 ml (10 fl oz)
bay leaves	3 medium

vital statistics

A powerhouse of iron, B vitamins and protein from the liver, and fibre and a massive helping of protective antioxidants from the richest of all sources, prunes. Combined with the antiviral and bacterial benefits of onions, and the rosmarinic acid in sage, which is anti-inflammatory, antiseptic and astringent, could you ask for a better protective recipe?

Served on a bed of herb-flavoured rice, this is a simple but showy dish. Make sure you use organic chicken livers to avoid antibiotics, and the best-quality prunes, preferably pruneaux d'Agen. If you can't get shallots, substitute pieces of red onion. When the recipe says fry in butter, it means it; for an occasional treat, the flavour bonus far exceeds the minimal health risk.

venetian kebabs

chicken livers 250 g (approximately 8 oz)

butter 25 g (approximately 1 oz)

shallots 12, peeled

brown-cap mushrooms 12 small

cherry tomatoes 12 small and firm

prunes 6, soaked, dried, pitted and halved

sage leaves 12, washed

1 Wash and dry the chicken livers. Fry in butter for no more than two minutes.

2 Remove livers with slotted spoon, but reserve the butter.

3 Cut each liver into three pieces and thread onto four long skewers with the remaining ingredients: a sage leaf, a liver, a prune, a shallot, a tomato, a mushroom, a sage leaf, and so on.

4 Brush each kebab with some of the reserved butter and cook under a very hot grill, turning frequently until done, approximately five minutes.

vital statistics

An apple a day may keep the doctor away, according to the proverb, but in truth it should be two, as they will supply sufficient fibre and natural plant chemicals to reduce cholesterol and blood pressure. Add the digestive and antiseptic volatile oils in mint and the antibacterial properties of cicely for an all-round protective sweet.

Nothing could be simpler than this delicious variation on traditional baked apples. The natural combination of mint and apple is enhanced by the intriguing hint of aniseed that is imparted by sweet cicely. Together with the added sweetness and succulence of the honey and butter, these herbs create a beguiling mixture of fragrance and flavour.

cicely surprise

apples 4, medium-sized, British dessert variety

mint 8 leaves

sweet cicely 1 teaspoon of finely chopped leaves

honey 4 teaspoons, runny

butter 4 very small knobs

1 Core the apples and discard each core, but ensure the bottom of each fruit remains intact.

2 Place each apple on a large square of foil and fill with mint leaves, a pinch of cicely, a teaspoon of honey and a knob of butter.

3 Wrap each apple securely in its foil.

4 Bake in a preheated oven at 180°C (350°F/gas mark 4) for 20 to 30 minutes, or until soft. (This recipe also works brilliantly on a barbecue.)

vital statistics

Plenty of calcium and vitamin D from whole milk makes this dish a good bone-protector. Borage is a useful sickroom herb as it reduces fevers and is soothing to the whole respiratory tract. It is also mildly diuretic and helps reduce fluid retention.

A better-than-average rice pudding that not only tastes good, but does you good, too. For a bit of extra dash, sprinkle a few pure, deep-blue borage flowers on top. This wonderful plant was much revered by the Moors in southern Spain, where it originates. Its heath benefits are listed above, but it does contains a toxic alkaloid and should not be eaten on a regular basis.

moorish rice pudding

whole milk	500 ml (16 fl oz)
borage	1 teaspoon shredded leaves
coriander	2 pinches crushed seeds
pudding rice	60 g (2 oz)
dried apricots	75 g (2.5 oz), chopped into small pieces
brown sugar	1 tablespoon

1 Put the milk, borage leaves and coriander into a saucepan. Bring slowly to the boil, then turn off the heat and leave until cool.

2 Strain the milk and pour into an ovenproof dish with the remaining ingredients.

3 Transfer to a low oven – 150°C (300°F/gas mark 2) – and leave for two hours, stirring occasionally during the first 45 minutes.

4 Serve hot or cold.

vital statistics

Elderflowers are traditionally used for the treatment and prevention of respiratory infections. They are also helpful for catarrh, hayfever and children's ear infections. In combination with mint, they are also useful for the relief of flu and its symptoms. Elder is reputedly a good anti-inflammatory, thanks to its content of ursolic acid, so it also helps relieve arthritis and rheumatism.

Whether you eat the rhubarb hot or cold with the yoghurt sauce, this makes a delightful combination. The delicate, scented taste of elderflower contrasts with the more astringent flavour of rhubarb, its acidity tempered beautifully by the creamy yoghurt. You can gather elderflowers for free from any hedgerow, but don't plant a tree in your garden unless you want a forest full!

flowery rhubarb delight

rhubarb	750 g (1 lb, 10 oz), washed and cut (2 cm/1 in pieces)
brown sugar	2 tablespoons (or to taste)
elderflowers	a handful of fresh flowers, well washed
natural yoghurt	1 x 600 ml (20 fl oz) carton, live
mint	4 chopped leaves plus 4 whole leaves to garnish
cinnamon	1 teaspoon
lemon	zest of half

1 Put the rhubarb and sugar in a large saucepan with just enough water to cover.

2 Place the elderflowers in a piece of muslin, tie into a bag and add to the rhubarb.

3 Cover and bring slowly to the boil. Simmer for ten to 15 minutes until cooked, stirring occasionally. Remove the bag of elderflowers.

4 Whisk together yoghurt, chopped mint, cinnamon and lemon zest.

5 Serve the rhubarb covered with yoghurt and decorated with remaining mint leaves.

power herbs

Total fitness is a mixture of stamina, strength and mobility. Whether you're eight or 80, this essential combination adds up to power – the power that allows you to use your physical and mental abilities when they're needed.

When thinking in purely physical terms, most people recognise that power is required for the instant energy used in explosive sports, a sprint for the bus or a mad cleaning spree just before the in-laws arrive. Yet power is equally essential when it comes to generating stamina for lengthy, sustained effort. An afternoon spent digging in the garden, a day of DIY or a physically demanding job: all these and other prolonged activities depend upon a slow and continuous flow of energy.

What many of us forget is that mental effort requires just as much power, whether you're taking a three-hour exam, sitting through a term of lessons and lectures, or doing a job that demands endless hours of concentration.

No matter what it is ultimately used for, however, the process of converting food into energy and energy into power demands good nutrition. Your brain and muscles need constant and instantly available supplies of blood sugar, and these can be achieved only by eating good food at regular intervals. For this reason, all the recipes in this section make use of natural sugars and complex carbohydrates to provide energy, and protein to boost muscle-building. In addition, all are made with power herbs that enhance these ingredients by aiding digestion and the absorption of nutrients as well as contributing their own individual benefits.

You'll already be used to cooking with popular herbs such as rosemary (for brain power and memory), sage (for mental stimulation and protection against infection) and bay (for its digestive benefits). You may even have used lavender on odd occasions for its tonic and anti-depressant properties; it's also great for headaches. But have you ever scattered pinks over a dish? Their tonic properties make them a brilliant invigorating herb as well as a colourful addition to desserts, providing a delicate, clove-like flavour.

With power herbs, you'll be able to try even more unusual plants, such as the strong, mint-flavoured pennyroyal, which improves digestion and absorption of nutrients, and southernwood, used since the Middle Ages as a bitter stimulating tonic. This aromatic herb not only acts as an energy booster, but it's a great insect repellent, too.

Wild chicory, marjoram and dandelion also make appearances in some of these unusual dishes, but whichever ones you choose – and I hope you'll try them all – you'll find them simple to make, good to eat and, of course, rich sources of natural power and energy.

cooking tip

Soaking anchovies in milk removes much of the salt and vinegar in which they're normally preserved. You could also use fresh, marinated anchovies, which are now more readily available and don't need to be soaked.

vital statistics

Rich in protein, essential fatty acids, fibre, calcium and iron. Southernwood contains the volatile oil abrotanin, which improves digestion and the absorption of nutrients.
Note to expectant mothers: Southernwood, like its close relative wormwood, should not be eaten during pregnancy. Its traditional use in folk medicine is to bring on menstruation.

The sharp, aromatic flavour of southernwood combines perfectly with the creaminess of mayonnaise and salty anchovies in this unusually delicious recipe. In addition, crunchy beans make a great foil for the soft, delicate eggs. As well as being a power herb, southernwood has been used since medieval times as a flea, moth and general insect repellent.

southernwood eggs

eggs 4, organic

anchovies 1 x 100 g (3½ oz) can or jar

whole milk 150 ml (5 fl oz)

mayonnaise 8 tablespoons home-made (or best commercial quality)

southernwood leaves 4 tablespoons, finely chopped

kidney beans 1 x 200 g (7 to 8 oz) can, rinsed thoroughly

1 Boil the eggs for ten minutes. Rinse immediately in lots of cold water and leave to rest for five minutes. Remove shells and cut in half lengthwise.

2 Soak the anchovies in milk for ten minutes. Drain.

3 Mix the mayonnaise with the southernwood leaves.

4 Arrange the egg halves on plates, surrounded with kidney beans.

5 Place the anchovies on the eggs in a criss-cross pattern and top with herb mayonnaise.

vital statistics

This really is a high power dish, offering brain-boosting protein from the fish and slow-release energy from the potatoes. It's also rich in essential fatty acids, zinc and selenium and very low in saturated fats. Sage provides thujone, flavonoids and bitters, so it acts as a tonic herb and hormone booster. Marjoram supplies eugenol, which stimulates the metabolism.

These delightfully light fish cakes are quick, easy to make, nutritious and inexpensive. The delicate taste of tuna is enhanced by the combination of sage and marjoram, making these a smart choice for everyone – particularly when served with a fresh, green salad. They're also excellent served cold, and they make a good carbohydrate/protein boost for athletes.

smart sage fish cakes

onion	1, medium, very finely chopped
tuna	1 x 250 g (8 to 9 oz) can
potatoes	250g (8 oz) roughly mashed
marjoram	1 teaspoon fresh, finely chopped (½ teaspoon dried)
sage	1 teaspoon fresh, finely chopped (½ teaspoon dried)
eggs	2 organic, beaten
olive oil	about 150 ml (5 fl oz), extra virgin

1 Sauté the onion gently in olive oil. Allow to cool and mix thoroughly with the tuna.

2 Add the potatoes and herbs and mix well.

3 Add half the beaten egg and mix again.

4 Form the mixture into eight flat cakes.

5 Dip each cake in the remaining egg.

6 Shallow fry gently in olive oil for seven minutes each side.

cooking tip

This dish goes brilliantly with olive oil mash. Choose a floury potato variety such as Golden Wonder, cook several whole to keep the healthy starch, then rub off the skins. Dice, put back in the saucepan and return to a gentle heat to dry thoroughly. Add extra-virgin olive oil, black pepper and parsley and mix thoroughly.

vital statistics

Bursting with minerals and beta-carotene from the root vegetables, and fibre, protein and other important carotenoids from the spinach or chard. Circulation-boosting phytochemicals from the garlic and onions mix with powerful liver-cleansing properties from the fennel. Rosemary's borneol, apigenin and rosmarinic acid produce tonic and anti-inflammatory properties and stimulate mental powers. Added stimulation comes from the cineole and laurenolide present in bay leaves.

Super-charged power radiates from this lovely lamb dish. What's more, even though it takes a few hours to cook, the preparation couldn't be simpler. The classic flavour of rosemary is sure to please, and it enhances the rest of the power nutrients contained in the vegetables and meat. And don't worry about leftovers: it tastes just as good cold for a quick lunch the following day.

robust rosemary lamb

1 Heat the oil and gently sweat onion and garlic. Remove from the pan.

2 Wash the lamb, dry thoroughly, season with salt and pepper and gently sauté it in the oil, sealing it all over.

3 Place into a large casserole dish along with the onion and garlic.

4 Add the vegetables, bay leaves, rosemary and stock to the casserole.

6 Bring gently to the boil, adding more water if necessary, then put into an oven preheated to 200°C (400°F/gas mark 4) for two hours, checking stock level occasionally.

7 Half an hour before dish is ready, add spinach or Swiss chard, making sure the leaves are covered with the stock.

olive oil	about 6 tablespoons, extra virgin
onion	1 large, chopped
garlic	2 cloves, chopped
lamb	4 chops or 8 cutlets, preferably organic, most of the fat removed
salt	to taste
black pepper	freshly ground, to taste
carrots	2, large, peeled and diced
turnips	4, baby, peeled and sliced
fennel	one bulb, cut into chunks
bay leaves	4 medium
rosemary	1 large sprig
herb stock	900 ml (30 fl oz)
spinach or swiss chard	500 g (about 1 lb), well washed and torn into shreds

growing tip

Pennyroyal isn't a herb you'll find on a supermarket shelf, but this hardy perennial grows well in a pot. The creeping variety is especially easy to grow, and boasts pretty spring flowers and a strong smell of peppermint to boot.

vital statistics

Rich in iron, B vitamins – especially B_{12} – and plenty of good energy calories from the rice. Volatile oils are provided by pennyroyal, particularly pulegone, menthol and limonene. Pennyroyal also contains bitter phytochemicals, which stimulate gastric juices and improve the digestion of meat.

A power-packed dish sure to please even the fussiest carnivore. Steak isn't a principal part of the Mediterranean diet, but when they do it, it's a veritable feast. Here, the combined flavours of the marinade and meat blend seamlessly with the garlic, sage and marjoram in the rice. It's made all the more interesting by the addition of the pungent, minty pennyroyal – but do use it sparingly.

mediterranean steak

beef 4 fillet steaks, preferably organic

red wine 300 ml (10 fl oz)

bay leaves 2 medium

onion 1 medium, chopped

garlic 2 cloves, chopped

olive oil 8 tablespoons, extra virgin

arborio rice 250 g (8 to 9 oz)

vegetable stock 500 ml (18 fl oz)

mixed herbs 1 tablespoon each of sage, parsley and marjoram,

pennyroyal 1 small pinch

1 Marinate the steaks in the wine with the bay leaves, half the onion, garlic and olive oil for one hour.

2 Sweat the rest of the onion and garlic in the remainder of the olive oil.

3 Add the rice and stir until coated.

4 Mix the herbs into the stock.

5 Add the stock gradually to the rice and simmer until each addition is absorbed.

6 Add the wine marinade, minus the bay leaves.

7 Grill or fry the steaks for five to six minutes each side, depending upon preference.

vital statistics

A feast of power-boosting iron comes from the liver, together with protein, vitamin B_{12} and a massive dose of vitamin A. This dish also provides a day's dose of vitamin C from the lime juice, all brilliantly digested thanks to the phytochemicals in wild chicory. **Note to expectant mothers:** avoid this dish due to its high vitamin A content.

growing tip

Sage is one of the easiest herbs to grow. You can get a plant, put it in a pot or in the garden, and as long as you prune it regularly (and you can freeze the leaves) it will last through most British winters. In summer, the flowers are beautiful, and are also delicious when floated on soups or added to salads.

The pink calves' liver contrasts beautifully with the bright green of the limes and the colours of wild chicory and blackened sage to make this dish as appealing to the eye as it is to the taste buds. Crisp, fried sage leaves are a perfect foil for the melt-in-the-mouth consistency of organic calves' liver – and the iron it provides (enhanced by the wild chicory) makes this a power dish extraordinaire.

lively chicory liver

sunflower oil	6 tablespoons
sage leaves	16 medium
butter	75 g (2 oz) unsalted, preferably organic
calves' liver	4 thin slices
wild chicory	4 teaspoons fresh leaves
limes	2, cut in half

1 Heat the sunflower oil and fry the sage leaves for around one minute, until crisp.

2 Drain the leaves on kitchen roll and keep warm.

3 Melt the butter in a frying pan. Sprinkle the liver with chicory leaves and cook for one minute on each side.

4 Serve scattered with the sage leaves, with the lime halves on the side.

growing tip

Bay trees can be very pricey in nurseries and garden centres, so for
cooking, don't choose the expensive plants trimmed into architectural
shapes; any healthy-looking bay bush is perfectly fine. They grow well, and
they'll survive most winters. If you're lucky enough to have a tree, you can
use the leaves fresh or hang a bunch in the kitchen to use dried.

A non-meat dish with the power punch of a mule, yet just reading the recipe conjures
up images of lazy, sun-drenched lunches in Spain, Portugal, Italy or southern France.
The unique flavour and texture of aubergine, the giant, misshapen tomatoes and the
ever-present smell of marjoram make this the perfect winter pick-me-up. It's delicious
hot or cold, and even your most carnivorous friends won't notice the absence of meat.

a taste of summer

1 Peel the aubergines and slice, sprinkle with a little salt both sides and put on an
oiled baking tin in a preheated oven at 200°C (400°F/gas mark 5) for ten minutes.

2 Sweat the onions and garlic in olive oil for ten minutes.

3 Cut the courgettes, mozzarella and tomatoes into medium-sized slices.

4 Pour the onion mixture into an ovenproof dish.

5 Layer with aubergines, then tomatoes, courgettes and mozzarella, finishing with a
mozzarella layer on the top.

6 Mix the crushed bay leaves, chopped marjoram, dandelion and raclette and
sprinkle over the top of the mozzarella.

7 Cover with aluminium foil, return to the oven and bake at 200°C
(400°F/gas mark 5) for 50 minutes.

8 Remove the foil and bake for a further ten minutes, or until slightly crisp.

vital statistics

Provides calcium from the two cheeses, protein, fibre and vitamins galore from the vegetables, extra iron and carotenoids from the dandelion leaves, heart-boosting lycopene from the tomatoes and the stimulating volatile oils from marjoram.

aubergines	2 medium
salt	a pinch or two, to taste
olive oil	150 ml (5 fl oz), extra virgin
onions	2 red
garlic	3 cloves, finely chopped
courgettes	6, large
mozzarella	450 g (1 lb), best-quality buffalo
tomatoes	4 beef, slicing variety
bay leaves	3 medium, crushed finely
marjoram	3 tablespoons, finely chopped
dandelion leaves	1 tablespoon, finely chopped
raclette	6 tablespoons, grated

Many amateur cooks avoid brûlées, thinking they're just too difficult to make. This recipe proves them wrong in the most delicious fashion. Cracking through the topping to uncover the succulent wine-flavoured pear adds to the pleasure of this indulgently energizing dessert, which is enhanced by the delicate flavour of lavender, a herb too often neglected in cooking.

lavender pears

pears	4 Comice, washed, peeled and halved
red wine	450 ml (15 fl oz)
eggs	3 yolks
flour	20 g (1 oz)
caster sugar	100 g (4 oz)
crème fraîche	500 ml (18 fl oz)
honey	50 g (2 oz) local, organic
lavender	10 heads

1 Poach the pears in the red wine for about 20 minutes. Pour off liquid.

2 Whisk the egg yolks, flour and half the sugar together.

3 Heat the crème fraîche, honey and lavender over a low heat, then sieve into the egg mixture.

4 Return to heat, and warm gently until thickened. Pour over fruit.

5 Sprinkle with the remaining sugar and heat under a grill until slightly burnt.

vital statistics

A perfect power pudding containing instantly available calories, along with fibre, carotenoids, iron and potassium from the dried fruit, bone-building calcium and protein from the yoghurt and mascarpone, and the immune-boosting friendly bacteria, also courtesy of the yoghurt. The European pink is famed for its general tonic properties.

cooking tip

Before using the pinks' petals, remove the small white spurs at the base of each, as they taste very bitter.

This wonderfully colourful compote is perfect as an unusual dinner-party dessert or a lazy, late Sunday breakfast. The clove-like flavour of the pinks melds beautifully with the spiciness of cinnamon. The idea of using pinks in cuisine may seem strange to the Western cook, but their Chinese relative, *Dianthus superbus*, has a culinary tradition dating as far back as the first century.

in the pinks

dried fruit 450 g (1 lb), mixture of apricots, mangoes, paw-paw, bananas, cherries or any other fruit you like

sweet white wine 300 ml (10 fl oz)

cinnamon stick 1

mascarpone cheese 200 g (7 to 8 fl oz)

live bio yoghurt 200 g (7 to 8 fl oz)

pinks 12 petals, torn into tiny pieces

1 Poach fruit gently in the red wine and cinnamon, adding just enough water to make the liquid cover the fruit.

2 Leave to cool, preferably overnight. Remove the cinnamon stick.

3 Mix the mascarpone and yoghurt thoroughly.

4 Stir in the pinks petals.

5 Spread the petal mixture on top of the fruit – and serve.

mood herbs

I'm always amazed by how little attention is paid to the mood-enhancing qualities of herbs and other foods. Naturopaths and herbalists have used this ancient knowledge for centuries – and now you can, too. Lavender may be used to induce sleep, a basil sandwich can help relieve anxiety. Rosemary can improve memory and concentration, while camomile and scented geraniums help overcome stress.

Nature's herbal pharmacy is every bit as potent as the man-made pharmaceutical industry. The most ancient civilisations developed powerful mood- and mind-altering medicines from the abundance of plants which grew where they lived, whether in the Brazilian rain forest, the islands of the Indian Ocean, the African continent or the oak-filled forests of ancient Britain. Today, in the 21st century, it is hard to believe that there are still natural medicines that can take the place of antidepressants, herbal teas to drink instead of sleeping pills, and plants that provide a natural high.

Yet herbs alone aren't the only substances that alter mood and mental outlook; the foods with which they are combined and the way these foods are prepared and eaten produce profound effects. For example, high-protein chicken paired with calming lemon balm and tarragon will raise mental energy and soothe frayed nerves before an exam or an important interview (*see* page 55). The Lavender Biscuits on page 61 blend the relaxing properties of this wonderful herb with carbohydrates containing tryptophan, a substance that releases relaxing hormones from the brain. Rosemary Salmon on page 56 is an effective memory-boosting dish, thanks to the rosemary's volatile oils. Rosemary has been used as a mind-booster since the time of the ancient Greeks, so it is no coincidence that it is often planted in gardens of remembrance.

In this chapter, you will also learn about the mood-enhancing qualities of coriander, oregano, fennel and the curry plant, as well as the common mint – all add different beneficial properties to the dishes they flavour. Even delicious desserts can exert a positive effect on mood. Aromatic Apples (see page 60), for example, deliver instantly available mental energy from fruit sugars, as well as protein and slow-release energy for sustained mental effort from the mascarpone cheese; the unusual addition of hyssop simultaneously stimulates mental activity and exerts a gentle overall calming action.

In addition to the recipes in the following pages, there are some general nutrition rules to bear in mind when striving for a balanced temperament. Foods such as oily fish, offal, lean beef, oats, barley, brown rice, dried and sprouted beans, apricots, blackcurrants, beetroot, shellfish, seeds and nuts are good aids to maximum all-round brain performance. Zinc is the key mineral needed for healthy brain function, and oysters are its richest source, but this mineral is also found in other fish, shellfish and pumpkin seeds. Lack of B vitamins may aggravate or even lead to depression, so you should be eating wholegrain cereals as well as all the other foods listed above.

Finally, if you want to achieve that positive 'I can do anything' feeling all day long, then maintain a balanced blood-sugar level in order to avoid the huge fluctuations that frequently trigger mood swings. Five or six small meals a day should be your regime instead of skipping breakfast, grabbing half a sandwich at your desk for lunch and having a huge meal late in the evening.

Enormously rich in beta-carotenes, this dish is a valuable protector against heart and circulatory disease and some cancers. Its mood-enhancing properties come from the eugenol in basil and the coriandrol from coriander.

I defy anyone who claims to hate 'boring old carrots' not to be captivated by this variation on a traditional soup recipe. The combined flavours of basil, coriander and the calcium-rich smoothness provided by the crème fraîche give this easily digestible soup a completely new dimension. A calming and effective feel-good dish that tastes great, too.

carrotiander soup

onion 1 medium, finely chopped

olive oil 2 tablespoons, extra virgin

carrots 900 g (2 lbs), finely cubed

basil ½ teaspoon dried, plus 10 large fresh leaves, roughly torn, for garnish

coriander ½ teaspoon dried, plus 5 fresh leaves, roughly torn, for garnish

herbal stock 1 litre (35 fl oz)

crème fraîche 250 ml (8 fl oz) carton

1 Sweat onion gently in oil for five minutes.

2 Add carrots and dried herbs, stir thoroughly and continue sweating for 15 minutes, stirring occasionally.

3 Pour in the stock, bring back to the boil and simmer until carrots are soft but not mushy.

4 Liquidize using a mouli or blender, or cool slightly, put through food processor and gently reheat.

5 Serve with a dollop of crème fraîche and garnish with fresh herbs.

vital statistics

Lemon balm is a traditional antidepressant and heart tonic, and the phytochemicals in tarragon are calming and sleep-inducing. The blood-building benefits of beetroot and pro-biotic bacteria from the yoghurt give this recipe added health-giving properties.

growing tip

Horseradish is seldom available fresh, but it's easy to grow your own. Be warned, however: once planted, it's almost impossible to get rid of, so put it in a large tub or contained bed at least two feet deep filled with a good, light soil and plenty of natural compost. Lift roots in the autumn, remove the thickest side shoots and store in damp sand for replanting in early March. (Country friends are bound to know where it grows wild.)

An unusual salad, with surprising mood-enhancing properties. This creamy, pink mixture brings a blaze of colour as an unusual starter, a light lunch dish served with wholemeal bread, a side dish with cold meat or fish or an accompaniment to a barbecue. It has the added piquancy of horseradish: a popular combination in Eastern Europe.

upbeet herbal salad

beetroot about 700 g (1 lb, 8 oz) cooked, preferably baby bulbs

lemon grated zest and juice of ½

horseradish 1 teaspoon fresh, grated (or 2 teaspoons ready-made sauce)

chives 1 heaped tablespoon, finely snipped

tarragon 1 teaspoon, finely chopped

lemon balm 1 teaspoon, finely chopped

natural yoghurt 1 x 250 ml (8 fl oz) tub, preferably live, bio variety

1 Cut the beetroot into chunks – or slice if large.

2 Sprinkle with the lemon juice and stir in zest.

3 Stir horseradish and herbs into the yoghurt and pour over the beetroot.

4 Leave for one hour to allow the flavours to combine.

The volatile oils in the rosemary act specifically on the brain, clearing muddled or tired heads. This recipe is also ideal for anyone with arthritis, gout or rheumatism, as it's rich in the essential fatty acids that have natural anti-inflammatory properties and are beneficial to the central nervous system. It is also an excellent source of protein.

When Grandma said fish was 'brain food', she wasn't kidding — especially when it's combined with the aromatic properties of rosemary. The essential fatty acids in oily fish are vital for human brain development, and since the time of ancient Greece, rosemary has been used as an all-round mental tonic. Besides aiding memory, it also helps lift depressive moods. Food for thought, indeed!

rosemary salmon

salmon 4 steaks

rosemary oil 2 tablespoons (*see* page 93)

lemon 8 thin slices

dried rosemary 4 generous sprigs

onion 1 medium, thinly sliced

dry white wine 2 tablespoons

1 Rub both sides of the fish with rosemary oil. Place in a baking tray lined with a piece of foil large enough to fold over the top of the fish.

2 Put two slices of lemon and a sprig of rosemary on each steak. Drizzle with a little more oil, surround the fish with the sliced onion and sprinkle with white wine.

3 Seal the foil parcel loosely and place in a preheated oven at 190°C (375°F/gas mark 5) for 20 minutes. Serve with minted boiled potatoes and any green vegetable.

High in **protein** and low in fat, duck breasts are a good source of **iron** and **B vitamins**. Rosemary's **volatile oils** enhance memory, anise provides **aphrodisiac** properties and saffron contains substances which lift the spirits. Both **linalool** and **borneol** in oregano are mood-enhancing.

chef's tip

This dish is great for barbecues, too. Simply wrap the duck breasts in foil, leave on the heat for ten to 15 minutes each side and serve with jacket potatoes.

A dish of unsurpassed mood food. The unusual combination of saffron and anise are a perfect complement to the rich meatiness of the duck – which tastes even better if it's wild. The memory-enhancing benefits of rosemary, the increased libido generated by anise and the general mood-improving properties of saffron make this the perfect meal to mend those lovers' quarrels.

canard aux herbes

duck breasts 4, skinned, preferably organic

olive oil 150 ml (5 fl oz), extra virgin

white wine or sherry vinegar 4 tablespoons

oregano 4 large sprigs

rosemary 2 large sprigs

anise 4 seeds, crushed

saffron 1 pinch

1 Remove any tendons from the duck breasts.

2 Mix together the rest of the ingredients and pour over the duck breasts. Leave to marinate for at least two hours.

3 Cook duck breasts under a high grill for seven minutes each side, basting frequently with the marinade.

4 Serve with mashed potatoes and French beans, sprinkled with parsley.

vital statistics

Bay has been used as a mood-improver since ancient times; its volatile oil, laurenolide, is a powerful mood-lifter. The fenchone present in fennel helps to regulate women's hormone levels, thus preventing mood swings. The combination of herbs with the essential fatty acids in the herrings makes this a perfect dish for affairs of the heart – emotional or physical.

The traditional combination of herrings with lemon, olive oil and fennel leaves is given a new and interesting twist in this recipe by the addition of curry plant and bay leaves. Due to its spirit-lifting effects, this makes a perfect meal if you're feeling a bit blue, but its nutritional value makes it equally good during pregnancy – and it's a four-star superfood if you're breastfeeding.

hearty herrings

olive oil 6 tablespoons, extra virgin

white wine vinegar 3 tablespoons

lemon 1, sliced

fennel 1 bunch of fronds

curry plant 6 leaves

bay leaves 2

herrings 4, filleted

herb mustard 2 teaspoons, tarragon flavoured

1 Mix together oil, vinegar, lemon, fennel, curry plant and bay leaves.

2 Season the fish fillets to taste, then pour over the oil mixture.

3 Cover and marinate in the fridge for at least three hours.

4 Drain the fish, wipe dry and shallow fry in olive oil for about four minutes each side.

5 Strain marinade and heat through. Add mustard to the marinade and pour over the fish to serve.

vital statistics

Rich in protein and B vitamins and a good source of iron, this recipe combines all the protective benefits of onions and garlic with the mood-enhancing essential oils of oregano and the mind-stimulating properties of mint.

Just to smell these cooking will transport you back to a Greek taverna in an unspoilt village – or make you yearn to visit this magical country if you haven't been there before. The traditional Greek way of cooking with lamb, herbs and spices creates an amalgam of wonderful flavours as well as a unique and mind-altering aroma.

minty lamb meatballs

lamb 700 g (l lb, 4 oz) lean meat, minced

onion 1, large, very finely chopped

garlic 2 cloves, very finely chopped

oregano 1 teaspoon, dried

mint 3 tablespoons finely torn fresh leaves

parsley 3 tablespoons flat-leafed variety, chopped

cumin 1 teaspoon

eggs 2 small

1 In a large bowl, combine the lamb, onion and garlic until thoroughly mixed. Season to taste.

2 Combine the oregano, mint, parsley and cumin and blend into the lamb mixture.

3 Beat the eggs and mix into the meat and herbs.

4 Form the mixture into walnut-sized balls (makes approximately 20) and refrigerate for one hour.

5 Transfer the meatballs into a greased baking dish. Cover with foil and cook at 180°C (150°F/gas mark 4) for 45 minutes. Remove foil.

6 Turn up the heat and cook for another ten minutes, shaking the dish until the meatballs are slightly crisp.

chef's tip
Keep a pot of scented geraniums growing all year round for a constant supply of fresh petals and leaves.

vital statistics
The aromatic oils in apples contain volatile substances which, when inhaled, act directly on the brain. Just smelling an apple can relieve migraines and lower blood pressure, so eating this combination is the ideal dessert to elevate your mood at the end of a meal. Used by the ancient Persians, advised by Hippocrates and mentioned in the Bible, hyssop is a naturally calming herb.

The tartness of the Bramley cooking apple is unique to the British Isles, and it is this acidity that mixes so well with the Mediterranean flavours of hyssop and scented geranium and the sweet smoothness of mascarpone cheese. This recipe makes a great breakfast dish, too, as well as being an ideal source of easily-digestible nutrients for anyone recovering from illness.

aromatic apples

water 100 ml (4 fl oz)

caster sugar 60 g (2 oz)

hyssop 1 sprig

bramley apples 900 g (2 lbs) peeled, cored and sliced

mascarpone cheese 500 g (approximately 1 lb)

scented geranium leaves 2 teaspoons, chopped

1 Pour the water into a saucepan. Add the sugar and hyssop and boil gently until the sugar is dissolved.

2 Remove the hyssop. Add the apples to the sugar mixture, cooking very gently over a low heat. When cooked to a smooth purée, fold in the mascarpone.

3 Place the mixture in individual dishes, sprinkle with geranium leaves and leave in the fridge to chill before serving.

The protein, vitamins and fibre in the flour and the tremendous calming effects of lavender make them a far better (and more enjoyable) alternative to sleeping pills or tranquillisers. Lavender oil is also a traditional remedy for the relief of headaches.

Most people associate its sweet aroma with the garden, but lavender is a great herb to use for flavouring food. Its ability to calm the nervous, relax the stressed and grant sleep to long-suffering insomniacs is legendary. Once you've tried these, you'll never want to eat bought biscuits again!

lavender biscuits

butter	115 g (4 oz)
caster sugar	55 g (2 oz)
75% wholemeal self-raising flour	175 g (6 oz)
lavender leaves	2 tablespoons, freshly chopped
lavender flowers	1 teaspoon, removed from stem

1 Cream the butter and sugar. Add the flour and lavender leaves and knead into a dough.

2 Roll onto a floured board, sprinkle with the flowers and press them into the dough with the rolling pin.

3 Cut into shapes and bake on a greased baking sheet at 230°C (450°F/gas mark 7) for about ten minutes.

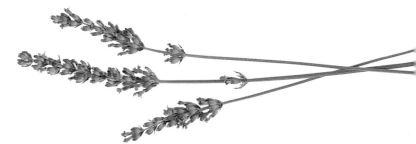

aphrodisiac

Say 'aphrodisiac', and you think of a magical substance which, within minutes of use, transforms a person into a state of burning passion and desire. Do such things really exist? I don't think so. Named after Aphrodite, Greek goddess of love and beauty, the true aphrodisiac is the love that draws couples together, whereas the mythical substances are merely bringers of lust, not love and jollity. Sadly, in today's world there is often a need for some outside help to improve both the quality and frequency of the physical expression of emotional involvement. This, yet again, is where Nature's own remedies come to man's – and woman's – aid. For the purposes of this chapter, I regard an aphrodisiac as any of the herbs, in combination with the right foods, that can exert beneficial effects on mind, body and spirit.

Until recently, the general consensus of medical opinion was that most sexual problems, male and female, were psychosomatic. While this is true in a small percentage of cases, many couples experiencing sexual difficulties do so because of a fundamental physical problem in either one or both. We've seen sperm counts halve in the last 20 years and fertility problems skyrocket, with both men and women experiencing difficulties. Male impotence is more common than ever, and female loss of libido is rapidly increasing. And what price the conventional treatment? Men rush to buy Viagra just to maintain an erection, despite the fact

herbs

that many deaths have already been attributed to this new drug; now it's being targeted at women, as the increased blood flow it produces can intensify and prolong sexual arousal.

Who or what is to blame for this 21st-century pandemic of sexual ills? Female hormones leaching into the water supply? Atmospheric pollution and toxic waste? Pesticides, insecticides, antibiotics and animal growth hormones in the food chain? Fast food and poor nutrition? The stresses of life in the fast lane for high-flyers and life at the sharp end for so many others? All of the above?

Of course, anyone experiencing sexual problems should see a physician. Yet, barring serious health problems, a little gentle aphrodisia can be found in the following recipes. They contain foods rich in essential nutrients which maintain and boost both physical and emotional arousal – herbs such as bergamot, coriander, nasturtium, rose petals, scented geraniums, rosemary and myrtle can all come to your aid. If you're planning a romantic dinner *à deux*, try some of these deliciously sensual dishes – and don't ignore the more unusual ones. If you're temporarily blinded in matters of love, they won't restore your sight, but they'll certainly do the job of a decent magnifying glass.

As in the other sections of this book, the recipes are meant to serve four people, but they'll all work equally well if you halve the quantities. On the other hand, why not invite a couple of friends round, help to rekindle their romance – and send them home early?

shopping tip
Though purslane has been eaten in Britain since the Middle Ages, you won't find it in the supermarket. It's hugely popular in north Africa, so ethnic shops which stock Moroccan or African foods will almost certainly sell it.

vital statistics
As well as protein, in surprising quantities for a vegetable, asparagus contains the strongly diuretic asparagine and asparagosides – a form of plant hormone – which may explain its reputation as an aphrodisiac. Purslane is one of the few plants that are rich in omega-3 fatty acids, making it a perfect romantic food for women.

Asparagus has been used as a medicine for around 3,000 years and is known to have been cultivated as a food plant in Egypt since 4000BC. Wherever it's grown, it has a reputation as an aphrodisiac. Eaten here with eggs (the ultimate symbol of fertility), vitamin E-rich walnut oil and the unusual flavour of purslane, it makes a dish Casanova would have been proud to taste.

cupid's spears

asparagus 24 spears, steamed and cooled

eggs 2 hard-boiled, cooled and chopped

purslane 110 g (3½ oz), roughly chopped

walnut oil and herb vinaigrette 6 tablespoons, (*see* page 95)

black pepper freshly ground, to taste

1 Arrange the asparagus spears on four plates.

2 Sprinkle the tips with egg.

3 Add a spoonful of purslane to each plate.

4 Drizzle the herb vinaigrette over the asparagus and the purslane.

5 Finish with a dash of black pepper – and draw the curtains.

vital statistics

Like all shellfish, prawns are rich in zinc, iodine and protein. Avocado is a generous source of heart-protective mono-unsaturated fatty acids and vitamin E, essential for sexual function and fertility. Coriander contains the volatile oil coriandrol and angelicin, and has been regarded as an aphrodisiac in Europe since the Middle Ages.

If you're old enough to remember the prawn cocktail of the '60s, you probably need help with your love life. This is it. Use the best prawns, a perfectly ripe avocado and, if you can't be bothered to make your own, a good commercial mayonnaise. This a real his'n'hers aphrodisiac: plenty of zinc for him, vitamin E for her and the side effects you'll both derive from coriander.

prawn avodisia

avocados 2 medium

Dublin Bay prawns 12, cooked

mayonnaise 8 large tablespoons

fresh coriander 3 tablespoons, chopped

1 Halve the avocados; remove the stones and peel.

2 Slice each half lengthways into six slivers.

3 Arrange the slices on four plates, along with the prawns.

4 Mix the fresh coriander with the mayonnaise and put two tablespoons on each plate.

Hallowe'en is a dreadful waste of pumpkins; such a nourishing vegetable deserves a better fate. This soup not only contains some vital ingredients for sexual function and fertility, it also has romantic eye-appeal. The peppery nasturtium contrasts deliciously with the oregano and curry plant, making an ideal start to a long, loving evening.

cinderella soup

1 Heat the oil and sweat the onions. Add the garlic and stir for two minutes.

2 Add the pumpkin and cook gently for two minutes, stirring to coat thoroughly.

3 Add the stock, curry plant leaves and oregano. Bring to the boil and simmer for 35 minutes.

4 Liquidize and reheat. Stir in the crème fraîche and wheatgerm, mixing thoroughly.

5 Serve with nasturtium flowers floating on top.

vital statistics

The phytochemicals in pumpkin are known for their gentle aphrodisiac effect. Vitamin E from wheatgerm and the circulatory benefits of garlic improve blood flow, and oregano has been valued since ancient times for its role as a stimulant. Nasturtium flowers contain glucocyanates, which are the substances responsible for Peruvian tribesmen's belief in its aphrodisiac powers.

olive oil	2 tablespoons, extra virgin
onion	1 large, sliced
garlic	1 clove, chopped
pumpkin	750 g (1 lb, 10 oz), peeled, deseeded and cubed
vegetable stock	1 litre (approximately 34 fl oz)
curry plant	2 teaspoons chopped leaves
oregano	1 teaspoon, dried
crème fraîche	250 ml (9 fl oz)
wheatgerm	1 tablespoon
nasturtium flowers	8, to garnish

chef's tip

If you can't find chard for this recipe, use spinach instead. Then there will be no need to remove the stalks.

vital statistics

Loads of energy-giving calories from the pasta combine with vitamin D and calcium from the goats cheese and beta-carotene from the chard. The essential oils in garlic specifically improve circulation, a benefit that is enhanced by similar properties in the onion, while the oregano helps calm any jangling nerves.

This unusual mixture of pasta, greens and goats cheese is light, full of energy and rich in potassium and calcium – essential for the prevention of cramp! Nervous tension can be a real 'downer' for men; when the vital moment comes, the calming effects of oregano should stave off disaster. Another love herb of the ancient world, oregano was said to be grown by Venus in her own garden of love.

a touch of venus

chard 200 g (7 oz), well washed, stalks removed and cut into strips, green parts roughly torn

red onion 1 sliced in thin rings

garlic 2 cloves, finely chopped

oregano a generous sprinkling of fresh leaves

olive oil 3 tablespoons, extra virgin

goats cheese 100g (3½ oz)

double cream 4 tablespoons

spaghettini 400 g (14 oz)

1 Sweat the chard stalks, onion, garlic and half the oregano in oil until the onion is soft.

2 Add chard (or spinach) leaves with a little water, stirring thoroughly. Cover and cook until wilted.

3 Beat together the cream, goats cheese, remaining oregano and pepper.

4 Drain the chard (or spinach) and add the goats cheese mixture to it. Stir thoroughly and keep warm until the pasta is cooked.

5 Pour the sauce over the pasta – and serve.

vital statistics

The easily digested protein and high mineral content of cod makes this a perfect romantic supper. The complex flavour of coriander comes from volatile oils, flavonoids and phenolic acids, which together produce the aphrodisiac effect. Saffron contains volatile oil and bitter glycosides, especially crocin. It also has carotenoids and vitamins B_1 and B_2, helps menstrual problems and indigestion and is reputed to be an aphrodisiac.

Extremely healthy, with classic visual, aroma and taste appeal, this dish is easily digestible and spiked with the aphrodisiacal properties of coriander and saffron. Widely used in Mediterranean countries, saffron's delicate flavour is of much greater value than the cheery yellow colour it gives to food (*see* above).

passionate poisson

olive oil	3 tablespoons, extra virgin
cod fillets	4
parsley	1 tablespoon, chopped
coriander	1 tablespoon, chopped
garlic	1 clove, finely chopped
saffron	½ teaspoon
stale wholemeal breadcrumbs	100 g (3½ oz)
lemon	juice of 1

1 Line an ovenproof dish with foil large enough to make a lid as well.

2 Brush the foil with oil.

3 Place fish fillets on the foil.

4 Mix the breadcrumbs, two tablespoons of the oil, parsley, coriander, garlic and saffron into a paste, adding more oil if necessary.

5 Spread over the fish and drizzle with lemon juice.

6 Fold over the foil and bake in a preheated oven at 190°C (375°F/gas mark 5) for 20 minutes.

7 Remove the foil and sear under a hot grill for one minute, or until brown.

Bergamot is a hardy perennial and grows easily – which is just as well because you won't find it in your local food shop. Many varieties have beautiful flowers which last all summer long. The best known is probably *Monarda didyma*, which will grow to about two and a half feet, so take care to plant it in a large pot.

Just the smells coming from the kitchen are enough to set the mood for a night of romance. The pungency of cider and thyme, the exotic aromas of cloves and nutmeg and the perfumed hint of bergamot… these should put anybody in a loving frame of mind.

exotic herbal chicken

1 Gently cook the onion in the olive oil for three minutes. Add the garlic, nutmeg, cloves and bergamot and cook for two more minutes.

2 Add chicken, cook gently, turning until brown all over.

3 Pour in the cider and vinegar and add the thyme. Simmer, covered, for 20 minutes.

4 Add the peppers and simmer for another 20 minutes until the chicken is cooked.

5 Remove the thyme, and serve surrounded by vegetables and covered in sauce.

vital statistics

A high-protein, low-fat dish, combining mood-enhancing nutmeg with its content of myristicin and cloves with their volatile oil eugenol (a powerful stimulant). The antiseptic thymol in bergamot was traditionally given as tea to new brides by North American Indians.

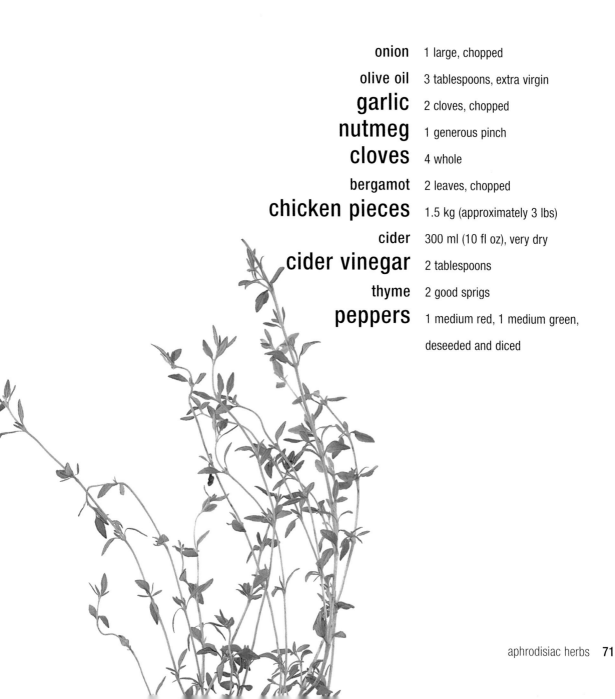

onion	1 large, chopped
olive oil	3 tablespoons, extra virgin
garlic	2 cloves, chopped
nutmeg	1 generous pinch
cloves	4 whole
bergamot	2 leaves, chopped
chicken pieces	1.5 kg (approximately 3 lbs)
cider	300 ml (10 fl oz), very dry
cider vinegar	2 tablespoons
thyme	2 good sprigs
peppers	1 medium red, 1 medium green, deseeded and diced

Protein, iron and B vitamins from the beef, with large amounts of vitamins A, C and E from the vegetables are all essential for a good love life. Zingiberene and gingerol in ginger stimulate and improve circulation – important for male performance. The volatile oils and flavonoids in rosemary also stimulate circulation. Myrtle provides myrtenol and cineole, both powerful tonics.

Certain romance writers maintain that only men who eat plenty of red meat make good lovers; certainly there has been a link between meat and virility since men were hunters. Ginger, rosemary and sesame seeds are regarded as aphrodisiacs all over the world, and myrtle – once dedicated to Aphrodite, goddess of love – adds the final touch. All, of course, impart superb flavour, too.

myrtle magic

sesame oil 2 teaspoons

peanut oil 2 tablespoons

sesame seeds 2 teaspoons

organic beef 400 g (12 oz) fillet, cut into thin strips

ginger 2.5 cm (1 in) fresh, peeled and grated

mixed stir-fry vegetables 400 g (12 oz)

myrtle leaves 6 medium

rosemary 1 teaspoon, finely chopped fresh leaves only

1 Heat both oils in a wok or large frying pan. When just beginning to smoke, add the sesame seeds and stir-fry for 30 seconds.

2 Add the meat and the ginger and stir-fry for three minutes.

3 Tip in the vegetables, myrtle leaves and rosemary. Stir-fry for two minutes. Remove from heat.

4 Serve with rice or noodles, and sprinkled with dark soy sauce, if desired.

This powerful aphrodisiac recipe contains huge amounts of iron and vitamin B_{12} from the liver, vitamin E from the almonds, crocin from the saffron and the spirit-raising rosmaricine in rosemary.

Several great 'love foods' are present here. In primitive societies, the liver was considered a guarantee of strength and virility. Almonds were renowned Middle Eastern aphrodisiacs, while rosemary was considered the herb of fidelity. In medieval times, saffron was believed to foster a happy heart. Amaretto, which adds its own heady aroma, completes this romantic dish.

lovers' liver

stale wholemeal breadcrumbs	100 g (3½ oz)
ground almonds	100 g (3½ oz)
garlic	1 clove, crushed
rosemary	1 tablespoon, leaves only, very finely chopped
saffron	2 generous pinches
black pepper	freshly ground, to taste
olive oil	3 tablespoons, extra virgin
butter	55 g (2 oz)
organic calves' liver	750 g (l lb, 10 oz) in 4 slices
amaretto	2 tablespoons

1 Mix the breadcrumbs, almonds, garlic, rosemary, saffron and lots of black pepper together with one tablespoon of the olive oil.

2 In a large skillet, heat the remaining oil with the butter, add liver slices and sauté for one to two minutes.

3 Turn and cook for a further one to two minutes.

4 Remove with a slotted server, set aside and keep warm.

5 Put the remaining ingredients in the pan to mix with the juices. Simmer briskly for one minute, stirring constantly.

6 Add the amaretto, simmer for one minute, and spoon over the liver to serve.

Turkey is an ideal high-protein meat, with practically no adverse effects on the coronary arteries. Phytochemicals from onions and garlic are equally heart-protective, with the added bonus of improving blood flow through the tiniest capillaries. The borneol in rosemary and other essential oils in oregano stimulate both mind and body, enhanced by the cineole in bay leaves. Xanthines and theobromine in the chocolate stimulate the brain to release natural hormones which trigger feelings of romance, love and desire.

Turkey is an extremely healthy food source, which is one reason it is widely eaten in North America all year round. This recipe, combining the stimulating effects of herbs, becomes a real aphrodisiac superstar when dark chocolate is added to the turkey – a savoury tradition that goes back centuries in South American countries, and tastes exotically delicious.

chocolate turkey with

1 In a large casserole, heat the oil and brown the turkey pieces lightly all over.

2 Add the shallots and half the garlic. Stir for two minutes.

3 Pour in the wine, add the herbs and tomatoes. Turn down the heat and leave to cook slowly.

4 Meanwhile, dissolve the chocolate in 100 ml (4 fl oz) boiling water. Add the chilli powder and remaining garlic. Stir thoroughly and pour into the casserole.

5 Replace the lid and continue cooking on a low heat until the turkey is falling off the bone, about one and a half hours.

6 Serve on a bed of rice, which has been cooked with half a teaspoon of saffron.

Not all chocolate is what it seems. For the best flavour, choose organic dark chocolate with a minimum of 70 per cent cocoa. You can now find it in virtually every supermarket. Although it costs a little more, the flavour and aphrodisiac qualities are worth every penny.

oregano

turkey drumsticks	8 medium
olive oil	4 tablespoons, extra virgin
shallots	8, whole
garlic	2 cloves, very finely chopped
red wine	150 ml (5 fl oz)
rosemary	1 large sprig
bay leaves	3 medium
oregano	½ teaspoon, dried
chopped tomatoes	1 large can
dark, bitter chocolate	30 g (1 oz)
chilli powder	¼ to ½ teaspoon, depending on taste

This delicate and fragrant dessert soup provides the exotic tastes of Earl Grey tea, which gains its perfumed flavour from bergamot. Mix this together with all the bacchanalian connotations of grapes and wine, and what better prelude could you wish for before a night of passion?

bergamot grape soup

white wine 450 ml (16 fl oz)

caster sugar 175 g (6 oz)

Earl Grey tea 3 bags

seedless white grapes 500 g (1 lb, 2 oz)

mint 15 leaves

1 In a large saucepan, boil together wine, sugar and tea bags until the liquid thickens.

2 Slice the grapes, and add to the wine mixture. Simmer gently for five minutes.

3 Remove the tea bags.

4 Serve sprinkled with finely chopped mint.

vital statistics

Like all citrus fruits, vitamin C is major constituent of grapefruit and lemons, but grapefruit has the added benefit of naringin, which prevents clotting and lowers cholesterol levels, thus improving circulation. Surprisingly, rose petals supply some important natural chemicals, including volatile oils which improve blood flow as well as being antidepressant and anti-inflammatory.

You may think the use of rose petals and rosewater in this dish is just for visual effect. They do make this sorbet look beautifully romantic and give it a wonderfully refreshing taste. Yet inhabitants of the Middle East have gathered rose flowers at the end of the summer for more than 3,000 years for their medicinal benefits – which have been highly regarded ever since.

pink passion

caster sugar 200 g (7 oz)

rosewater 250 ml (8½ fl oz)

pink grapefruit juice 350 ml (12 fl oz)

lemon juice 3 tablespoons

pink grapefruit 1, cut into segments, with rind, pith and pips removed

rose petals 1 handful

1 Boil sugar and rosewater for four to five minutes. Cool.

2 Mix together the grapefruit and lemon juices.

3 Combine the juices with the sugared rosewater, pour into a freezer-proof dish and freeze until almost firm.

4 Break into chunks and reduce to a slush in a food processor, or put into bowl and use a mouli.

5 Return to the freezer, cover and freeze until firm.

6 Serve several mounds on each plate, with the grapefruit segments arranged around the side and rose petals scattered over the top.

growing tip

Most people love the look of sunny geranium flowers, but why not plant a few of the scented variety? They're perfect on a patio or near a bedroom window, where their sensual aromas can work their magic. There's no mystery to scented geraniums for cooking; they're available at garden centres all over the country. Jekka McVicar, the doyenne of herb growing, recommends the rose geranium (*Pelargonium graveolens*), a half-hardy evergreen perennial, which is perfect for cooking.

vital statistics

Plums are a rich source of beta-carotene, vitamins C and E and malic acid, which together promote a healthy heart and good circulation. The aromatic leaves of scented geraniums contain calming volatile oils, widely used in aromatherapy for reducing stress.

The luscious English Victoria Plum is one of the world's great fruit treats. It's not just the flavour that makes it a national treasure, but its all-round health benefits. With a scant dab of butter and hardly any sugar divided among four generous portions, this dessert will leave you guilt-free and licking your lips with delight and desire.

scented plums

butter 30 g (1 oz)

honey 3 tablespoons

red plums 8, just ripe

scented geranium leaves 4 torn, 4 whole for garnish.

sweet white wine 300 ml (10 fl oz)

caster sugar 1 tablespoon

1 Put the butter in an ovenproof dish large enough to hold halved plums in one layer. Heat gently until melted.

2 Stir in the honey and heat until runny.

3 Halve the plums, remove the stones and set, cut side down, on butter mixture

4 Add the torn geranium leaves to the wine and pour over the plums. Sprinkle with sugar.

5 Cook, uncovered, in a preheated oven at 180°C (350°F/gas mark 4) for 25 minutes, until plums are soft.

6 Serve decorated with whole geranium leaves.

vital statistics

Figs provide beta-carotene, iron, potassium and ficin, a digestive aid. Yoghurt is a rich source of calcium, and angelica contains volatile oil, lactones and coumarins, which make it an effective circulatory stimulant, improving blood flow to the extremities.

growing tip

You'll find crystallised angelica in any food shop; fresh leaves are more difficult to locate, so why not grow your own? Angelica is a large plant – up to six feet tall with a three-foot spread. It will, however, grow well in a large pot, with a stake to keep it upright. Give it plenty of water and harvest the leaves from spring onwards.

From India to the Middle East, ancient Greece to the modern Mediterranean, fresh figs have been a traditional symbol of love and sexual prowess. Angelica is often confined to the crystallised green bits used in cakes, but the real treat lies in its leaves: they have a delicate, sweet aromatic flavour, which, combined with the figs, makes this a heavenly dish indeed.

angel's kiss

ready-made puff pastry	1 sheet, completely defrosted
figs	8 medium, ripe and quartered
natural yoghurt	300 ml (10 fl oz)
brandy	1 tablespoon
caster sugar	60 g (2 oz)
eggs	2, large
angelica	2 tablespoons chopped leaves

1 Use the pastry to line a greased 8 x 11 inch oblong loose-bottomed tart tin.

2 Arrange the quartered figs on the pastry.

3 Beat together the yoghurt, brandy and all but two tablespoons of sugar.

4 Beat the eggs and add to the yoghurt mixture. Stir in the angelica leaves.

5 Pour the yoghurt mixture over the figs and sprinkle over with remaining sugar.

6 Bake in a preheated oven at 200°C (400°F/gas mark 6) for 30 to 40 minutes until risen, firm and dark, golden brown. Don't worry if it falls after cooling; the flavour stays great!

cleansing

'Cleanliness is next to godliness' is one of the most familiar English proverbs. In my opinion, however, it should read: 'Cleanliness is next to *healthiness*, which is next to godliness.' But take note: by cleanliness, I'm not referring to the modern epidemic of hygiene terrorism that is attempting to eliminate all bacteria (good or bad) from our homes, offices, gardens and, worst of all, our food. We need exposure to some bugs in order to build up a strong and protective immune system. The cleanliness that should be our major concern is inner cleanliness. With the best will in the world, most normal people enjoy the occasional bout of over-indulgence. Too much rich food, excessive consumption of alcohol, endless cups of tea and coffee and countless chocolates all work to clog up an otherwise efficient system.

Still, let's get one thing straight: life is for living and enjoying. This book is not another set of commandments from 'the food police' – not another attempt to remove all pleasure from the wonderful act of eating. This cleansing section is included as a guide to compensating for an abundance of enjoyment. These particular recipes have been designed to put the least possible strain on the body's eliminative and cleansing organs, the liver and kidneys, by incorporating herbs from Nature's pharmacy which encourage and speed the purifying process.

Anise, for example, has volatile oils that overcome the digestive discomforts of excess; as a bonus, it also has aphrodisiac qualities. In combination with peaches (*see* page 91), it makes a delicious light dessert, rich in skin-healing beta-carotenes. Basil,

herbs

which stars on page 84, is one of the most cleansing culinary herbs, of particular value for kidney and urinary problems and bursting with antibacterial power. Don't turn up your nose at Weed Soup (page 82); nettles and dandelions may seem unlikely and unappetising treats for the dinner table, but they're delicious and powerfully eliminating. Dandelion is a wonderful diuretic and nettles are a rich source of vitamin C and restorative chlorophyll.

Catmint, well known for its intoxicating effect on felines, is much less known for its cleansing properties. It helps lower high temperatures, relieves the symptoms of colds and flu and, combined in the chicken recipe on page 86 with the anti-inflammatory and antibacterial effects of rosemary, makes a great detox dish. The benefits of juniper berries are not confined to gin alone: they're another cleansing, eliminating and diuretic herb whose taste is a perfect match for the fish recipe on page 89.

By using these recipes exclusively over a three- or four-day period, you will create a simple detox plan that can be repeated regularly after periods of conspicuous over-consumption. Even just including a dish or two from this section on a regular basis will help keep your liver, kidneys and digestive system working at their optimum levels. None of the food in this section is a penance, however, so there is no need to put on a hair shirt before contemplating its preparation or consumption. Like all the recipes in this book, those made with cleansing herbs are designed to make consuming the richest herbal health benefits a most enjoyable experience.

growing tip

You won't find salad burnet in your supermarket, but it's easy to grow your own. It will do well in a pot and, being evergreen, is a constant source of delicious flavours throughout the winter. Keep cutting back to no more than 20 cm (eight inches) to encourage new leaf production.

vital statistics

Contains iron, potassium, folic acid, carotenoids and vitamin C. Dandelion is a powerful diuretic and a rich source of coumarins, relieving fluid retention and high blood pressure. Sorrel is a traditional herbalists' detox plant, whose tannins and volatile oils are good for the skin. Salad burnet aids digestion, and its delicate flavour is perfect in soups and salads.

Gardeners might have other ideas, but a 'weed' is really just a plant growing where it's not wanted. In this recipe, you'll want as many edible weeds as you can find, because they're nutritious as well as having therapeutic and cleansing benefits. The same basic method will work for all delicate, leafy herbs, preserving their flavours as well as their attractive green colour.

wonderful weed soup

mixed 'weeds':	90 g (3 oz), stemmed
dandelion, nettles, sorrel,	and well washed
rocket and salad burnet	
unsalted butter	45 g (1½ oz)
olive oil	2 tablespoons, extra virgin
onion	1, small, peeled and chopped
potatoes	175 g (6 oz)
herb stock	1 litre (approximately 34 fl oz)
crème fraîche	225 ml (8 fl oz)

1 Purée the 'weed' leaves in a food processor. Add the butter and purée again; set aside.

2 Sweat the onion gently in the oil. Add the potatoes and cook gently until golden.

3 Add the stock and simmer until the potatoes are soft. Stir in the crème fraîche and purée again.

4 Just before serving, whisk in leaves and butter.

vital statistics

Unpeeled courgettes are a valuable source of beta-carotene, essential for the skin during any cleansing programme. Parsley provides calcium as well as diuretic volatile oils, which speed fluid elimination. Chives enjoy the cleansing and detoxing properties of their relatives, garlic and onions, though with a less strident flavour.

Give this dish to the most dedicated meat-eaters, then let them tell you vegetarian food is boring! Apart from its cleansing benefits, it's a truly tongue-tingling mixture of flavours, especially the delicate overtones of aniseed from the chervil. Chervil's blood-purifying properties are part of ancient herbal folklore: it has been regarded as a traditional spring tonic for centuries.

chervil courgette bake

olive oil	3 tablespoons, extra virgin
courgettes	8, small
plum tomatoes	300 g (10½ oz) plump
garlic	1 clove
mixed herbs	4 tablespoons of any fresh,
(coriander, chervil,	succulent, chopped leaves
chives, parsley, etc)	
lemon	½, thinly sliced
salt	to taste
black pepper	freshly ground, to taste

1 Cut the courgettes lengthwise and deseed.

2 Peel, deseed and dice the tomatoes.

3 Rub an oven-proof dish with the garlic, then stir in the chopped herbs and tomatoes.

4 Place courgettes on top of the tomatoes and herbs, then cover with the lemon slices.

5 Season, cover with foil and bake in a preheated oven for about 20 minutes at 200°C (400°F/ gas mark 6), until courgettes are soft but not mushy.

A super-cleansing recipe. Cynarin from artichokes detoxifies the liver, while parsley provides a diuretic effect. The ultimate purifying benefits of garlic, the slow-release sugar, inulin (also from the artichokes), and the calming properties of basil give this dish additional health-enhancing qualities

The complex flavours of basil, chives and garlic are the perfect way to bring out the unique taste of artichoke hearts. Most of the recipes in this book are for fresh produce, but unless you're an expert – or have the whole day to spare – preparing a pile of fresh artichoke hearts is a thankless task. Just this once, save yourself trouble by buying the best-quality tinned ones you can find.

basil's brush

white wine	450 ml (16 fl oz)
garlic	6 cloves, chopped
parsley	225 g (8 oz)
chives	125 g (4½ oz)
plum tomatoes	3, large, chopped
olive oil	125 ml (4 fl oz), extra-virgin
artichoke hearts	2 x 350 g (12 oz) tins, drained
basil	5 tablespoons of leaves, snipped

1 In a large saucepan, boil the wine with the garlic for about three minutes.

2 Chop the parsley and chives and add to the pan.

3 Add the tomatoes, oil and artichokes and simmer until the artichokes are soft – about 15 minutes.

4 Just before serving, stir in the basil leaves.

5 Serve with some good, coarse bread for mopping up the sauce.

vital statistics

This low-fat, high-protein dish is a good source of calcium and vitamin C. The flavonoids and anthraquinones make sorrel a cleansing diuretic. Oregano is rich in carvacrol and thymol, making it antifungal and antibacterial. And if you use chervil, its volatile oils are diuretic and blood-purifying.

Organic veal is free from antibiotics, growth hormones and unwanted chemicals, but the delicate flavour of the escalope sitting on its bed of soft green sorrel is reason enough to eat this dish. The bonus is that you can include it in any cleansing or detox regime.

sorrel surprise

veal escalopes 4, beaten thinly

olive oil 6 tablespoons

lime juice from 1 fresh lime

oregano or chervil 2 tablespoons

salt to taste

black pepper freshly ground, to taste

butter 3 oz, unsalted

onion ½, very finely chopped

sorrel 6 oz, roughly torn

plain yoghurt ½ small carton (about 60 ml/2 fl oz)

1 Marinate the escalopes in olive oil, lime juice, half the chervil or oregano and seasoning for at least two hours.

2 Remove the veal from the marinade, and under a medium-hot grill, cook for about five minutes each side.

3 While the veal cooks, melt the butter in a saucepan, add the onion and cook gently until soft.

4 Add the sorrel, the rest of the oregano or chervil and wine. Cook until the sorrel is wilted – about four minutes.

5 Pour in the yoghurt and heat gently. Put the sauce onto plates and top each with an escalope.

A protein-rich cleansing dish that is also highly protective, thanks to the antioxidants in the root vegetables. Swedes and carrots are particularly rich in beta-carotene, and the apple provides the cholesterol-lowering fibre pectin. Catmint offers a storehouse of volatile oils, particularly citronellol, geraniol, thymol and lactones, which stimulate sweating, help lower temperature and make this dish ideal for those recovering from coughs, colds and flu.

One of the simplest main courses ever: all the vegetables cook with the meat, while the apples, cider and herbs give the most delicious flavour to the vegetables, particularly the potatoes. Catmint, also known as catnip, is rich in volatile oils, which are as delicious as they are purifying. Felines can get tipsy on it, but as a cleansing herb for humans, it's definitely the cat's meow!

tipsy catmint chicken

chicken portions	4, preferably free range
root vegetables	(must include potatoes) about 450 g (1 lb) of your favourites, cut into cubes
cooking apples	1 Bramley, peeled, cored and cut into cubes
rosemary	1 large sprig
catmint	3 large sprigs
cider	600 ml (20 fl oz)

1 Wash and dry chicken pieces.

2 Put all ingredients together in a large casserole dish.

3 Cook in a preheated oven at 200°C (400°F/gas mark 6) for two hours – and enjoy!

The antiseptic and antibacterial essential oils thymol (from thyme), and linalool, terpinene and eugenol (from marjoram) combine with the detoxing properties of chives to make this a quick-and-easy inclusion in your cleansing regime.

Simple, delicious and economical, this is a great supper dish at any time, in spite of its cleansing and detoxifying ingredients. You certainly don't have to be ill to enjoy it, but its high energy content also makes it a perfect food for convalescents.

nutty herb noodles

noodles	450 g (1 lb)
olive oil	3 tablespoons, extra virgin
cooked chicken	225 g (8 oz), cubed
or ham	or shredded
pine nuts	50 g (1¾ oz)
mixed herbs	2 tablespoons,
(marjoram, basil,	finely chopped
thyme, chives)	
parmesan	3 tablespoons, grated

1 Cook the noodles according to directions on the packet.

2 Heat the olive oil; add the ham or chicken and sauté gently.

3 Toast pine nuts in a dry frying pan for two minutes.

4 Add the noodles and the pine nuts to meat mixture.

5 Stir in the herbs, and serve with Parmesan.

growing tip

Both summer and winter savory grow wellpots, summer savory as an annual and the winter variety as a perennial. Winter savory is more common in Britain, where its hot, peppery flavour goes well with strong meats.

vital statistics

Pork is an excellent source of protein, iron and B vitamins. Onions help lower cholesterol, while fennel's volatile oils anethole and fenchone stimulate the liver and the digestive tract. The pinenes, borneol and carvacrol in winter or summer savory help fight infections, and as an added bonus, summer savory also helps to prevent flatulence.

Low-fat, high-protein organic pork makes Fennel Fillet a healthy addition to your menu collection. Add the cholesterol-lowering and antibacterial effect of onions and the purifying properties of fennel, and you have a cleansing, liver-stimulating and anti-inflammatory meal that – thanks to the unusual combination of fennel and savory in the creamy sauce – tastes terrific, too.

fennel fillet

pork fillets 1 kg (2 lbs, 2 oz), lean organic

olive oil 3 tablespoons, extra virgin

onion 1 small, finely chopped

flour 1 tablespoon, plain

white wine 150 ml (5 fl oz)

yoghurt or crème fraîche 200 ml (7 fl oz)

fennel and savory 1 teaspoon of each, finely chopped

1 In a skillet, brown the pork fillets in the olive oil.

2 Reduce the heat, cover and cook through, about 20 minutes.

3 Remove the meat, keep warm and pour off all but three tablespoons of fat.

4 Add the onion and sweat gently. Blend in the flour and add the wine.

5 Stir until thickened, add the yoghurt or crème fraîche, then the herbs.

6 Pour the mixture over the meat and serve.

Fish provides easily digested protein and a rich supply of minerals, including iodine. Juniper is rich in the diuretic and anti-inflammatory volatile oils myrcene, sabinene, pinene and limonene. The sulphur compounds in garlic and Welsh onion fight bacteria and fungal diseases, while the diuretic benefits of parsley add to this dish's cleansing properties.

The traditional use of juniper as a diuretic and anti-inflammatory is one reason for its inclusion in this recipe; its strong, tangy flavours and those of Welsh onions and garlic are another. Together, these herbs perfectly complement the tender white flesh of the sea bass, making this a mouthwatering way to cleanse the system.

juniper fish

welsh onion	2 tablespoons green leaves, finely chopped
garlic	3 cloves, minced
juniper berries	1 tablespoon, crushed
parsley	2 tablespoons, chopped
white wine	675 ml (24 fl oz)
sea bass	2 whole
olive oil	extra virgin
lemon	1, sliced

1 Mix the Welsh onions, garlic, herbs and wine.

2 Place the fish in a large baking dish and brush with olive oil.

3 Pour the wine and herb mixture over the fish.

4 Cover with sliced lemon.

5 Bake in a preheated oven at 220°C (450°F/gas mark 7) for about 30 minutes, basting frequently.

vital statistics

Cherries are super-rich in vitamin C, potassium, magnesium and a host of cancer-fighting phytochemicals. When combined with lemon verbena's volatile oils — limonene, geraniole and citral — they make a valuable addition to any cleansing regime, gently calming the digestion and pepping up the nervous system.

This exquisite variation on the classic Provençal *clafouti* is all the more delicious due to the combination of the slightly acidic cherries and the sweet, lemon-scented fragrance of verbena. This recipe also works well with any fresh stone fruits, such as plums, peaches and fresh apricots.

verbena delight

cherries 500 g (approximately 1 lb), washed, stones removed

lemon verbena 3 tablespoons, finely chopped

eggs 4, free range

caster sugar 60 g (2 oz)

flour 50 g (approximately 2 oz)

crème fraîche or cream 300 ml (10 fl oz)

brandy 3 tablespoons

1 Put the cherries in a buttered gratin dish. Sprinkle over with lemon verbena.

2 Whisk the eggs, stir in sugar, then slowly mix in flour.

3 Add crème fraîche (or cream) and brandy; stir until well mixed.

4 Pour the egg mixture over the cherries and herbs and bake in a preheated oven for 30 minutes at 180°C (350°F/gas mark 4).

As with all treats, these are a bit naughty, but the protein, vitamins and fibre in the flour and the tremendous calming effects of lavender make them a far better alternative to sleeping pills or tranquillisers. Just making these delicious nibbles is therapeutic, since the aromatic oils pervade your kitchen.

Few desserts can be enjoyed as part of a cleansing regime, but this one certainly fits the bill, as its flavours are as good as its cleansing properties. The surprising combination of catmint and anise brings out the subtle flavours of the peaches, resulting in a seemingly indulgent but nonetheless health-giving dish.

anise peaches

caster sugar 5 tablespoons

water 300 ml (10 fl oz)

star anise 3

peaches 4, large, peeled and sliced

catmint 4 sprigs

1 Heat the sugar with water over a low heat until dissolved.

2 Add the star anise and simmer gently for seven minutes.

3 Add peaches and continue simmering for ten to 12 minutes.

4 Remove the fruit and place in a ceramic heat-proof dish large enough to contain them in a single layer. Reduce the liquid by half.

5 Pour over the fruit and serve garnished with sprigs of catmint.

herbal drinks

Fresh or dried herbs can be made into enjoyable drinks consumed for pleasure alone. They can also be drunk to promote good health or to treat specific ailments. Most are made from leaves, though some seeds can also be used.

Take time for tea

To make herbal teas, you can use a glass (the best for fresh mint tea) or brew them straight into a cup or teacup. Ideally, however, it's best to use an infusion pot designed for the purpose, as they have built-in strainers to keep bits of bark or leaves out of your drink. The standard quantity used for making all herb teas is two heaped teaspoons of fresh herb, or one level teaspoon of dried, to a cup of boiling water. For the average teapot, the measure is two tablespoons of fresh, or four teaspoons of dried herb.

Herb teas take time to brew in order to extract their essential components, so cover them and leave to stand for five to ten minutes. The most popular choices are made from camomile, mint, lemon balm, lemon verbena, sage, sweet cicely, rosemary or bergamot. Adding honey, lemon or both enhances the flavour of most of these teas. For specific therapeutic properties, *see* 'the herbal pharmacy', page 110.

You can also combine the health-giving benefits of yoghurt with the therapeutic value of herbs via the Indian drink known as a lassi. This libation can be made either sweet or sour. Simply mix equal quantities of yoghurt and cold water with a tiny pinch of salt or a teaspoon of honey and add a few chopped leaves of sage, mint, lemon balm, anise, hyssop, sweet cicely or coriander. Chill well before drinking – and enjoy!

Make a tonic tipple

One of the nicest ways to reap the benefit of tonic herbs is by making your own tonic wine; fortunately, it's a simple process. All you need is a lidded jar with a tap on the bottom, and these can usually be obtained from chemist chains or winemaking shops. Wash and dry your chosen herb or mixture of nettles, rosemary, southernwood, sweet cicely or angelica. Place the herbs in the jar and add red wine (of reasonable quality), enough to cover the herbs completely. Stir gently with a wooden spoon, then make sure the lid fits tightly and leave to stand in a cool, dark place for at least four weeks. For your health's sake, enjoy a glass daily, but be sure to top up the wine before the herbs are exposed to the air. When the flavour weakens, strain off the herbs, reserving the liquid, and start the process again.

herbal oils and vinegars

Traditionally, herbal oils and vinegars were made when fresh plants were available so that their enhancing and enlivening flavours could still be enjoyed during the cold, bleak winter months. Today, however, practically every conceivable herb is available in dried form, which means that modern cooks can create oils and vinegars – and, of course, delicious dishes – with them all the year round. More importantly, however, the best reason for making fresh herbal oils and vinegars is to benefit from all their health-giving properties that can improve the body, mind and spirit.

They're simple to make and infinitely cheaper than commercially available varieties – many of which, I fear, are frequently made with chemically identical flavours and perfumes rather than real herbs.

Herbal oils

The same method is used to make all herbal oils, whether savoury or sweet; only the type of oil used varies, and the herbs change according to taste and purpose (*see* details below for specific oil qualities and page 94 for therapeutic mixtures). Flavouring is very much a personal matter, so all quantities are approximate and may be varied to suit your own palate.

It's best to make small quantities so that your oils are used before they go rancid, which all oil does, given time. Unless made with old oil, however, these health-giving mixtures will keep perfectly well for six months. Once prepared, pour into dark-coloured bottles, or cover with foil, and store in a cool place out of sunlight – but not in the fridge.

Extra virgin olive oil is used to make salad dressings, marinades, pasta, rice, grills, barbecues and dishes which don't need prolonged or very hot frying.

Rape-seed oil (known as canola in the US) is by far the healthiest oil for frying as it has the ideal balance of omega-3 and omega-6 fatty acids; alternatively, you can use peanut oil for dishes which need prolonged or deep frying.

Cold-pressed grape seed or almond oil is used in making sweet dishes, and is especially good for marinating fruit.

Basic method: rosemary oil

Rosemary oil can be used in power, aphrodisiac, cleansing and mood recipes. It goes well with lamb, poultry and pasta salads.

Oil 250 ml (5 fl oz)

Rosemary 1 tablespoon fresh leaves.

1 Put the leaves in a mortar with a little of the oil and crush gently with a pestle to release the flavours.
2 Add to the rest of the oil and pour into a tight-fitting screw-top jar. Leave on a sunny window-sill for three weeks, shaking gently every day or so.
3 Strain through muslin and pour into a bottle with a tight-fitting stopper, adding a sprig of fresh rosemary for aesthetic effect.

Other recipe suggestions

- Use garlic, basil or tarragon singly to make savoury oils.
- Lavender, scented geraniums, rose petals, mint or sweet cicely are good choices for sweet oils.
- A combination of thyme, sage, garlic and coriander (protective, cleansing and mood-enhancing, respectively) works well in marinades and casseroles; also for roasting chicken.
- Coriander, fennel, tarragon, oregano, parsley, dill, sweet marjoram, lemon thyme, southernwood and bergamot all make good oils on their own or in combinations to suit your taste.
- With the rise in popularity of wok cooking, you can also add herbs – particularly garlic, coriander, dried citrus peel, basil and lemon grass – to sesame, walnut or pistachio oils for use in stir-frying.

Creative containers

Get creative with your containers by purchasing unusual or decorative bottles and attractive labels for your home-made oils. These will allow you to create inexpensive yet impressive (and very welcome) gifts for the foodies you love. Add some ribbon or a strip of raffia around the neck of the bottle for an extra decorative touch.

Herbal vinegars

Just as with herbal oils, it's the combination of flavour and therapeutic value that makes herbal vinegars so interesting. Once made, they'll keep for months as long as the herbs are covered with vinegar; just top up the bottles as necessary. When the flavours get too weak, strain the vinegar into another bottle and start the process again. For cooks in a hurry, these vinegars can also be a time-saver, as you can add the taste of herbs without having to gather, wash or prepare them. They're also perfect for salad dressings, vinaigrettes or marinades and (added sparingly) to gravies and sauces.

Personally, I prefer vinegars made with single herbs, but whatever you choose to create, always use the best-quality cider or white-wine vinegars. Thankfully, the fashion for balsamic vinegar with everything is waning; delicious though it is, its flavour is too overpowering for many delicate dishes. Yet if you want to use it, buy the best you can afford and be very selective about how you use it.

Basic method

There are more complicated ways of making herb vinegars, but this is the simplest and it works very well.

1 Decant the cider or white-wine vinegar into a bottle with a largish neck and an airtight stopper.
2 Choose your leaves, petals, flowers or seeds. Wash if necessary and dry thoroughly.
3 Bruise gently in a mortar or with the back of a wooden spoon. Seeds should be partially crushed.
4 Put herbs in the vinegar, stopper tightly and leave for three weeks or so before using.

Suggested herbs for savoury vinegars

Dill or fennel Both are cleansing and mood-enhancing; and their vinegars are good with fish.

Garlic For protection, cleansing and as an aphrodisiac. Garlic vinegar goes with almost everything.

Mint For protection and as a digestive aid. Mint vinegar is wonderful with cold lamb, potato salad and in tabouleh.

Coriander seeds (1 tablespoon per 5 fl oz) Another aphrodisiac, also cleansing, digestive and mood-enhancing. Coriander vinegar tastes great on bean salads and in coleslaw.

Tarragon For protection and mood enhancement. Tarragon vinegar is brilliant in chicken gravy, on chicken salad and fish dishes.

Sweet vinegars for use in desserts can be made from rose petals, elderflowers, nasturtium flowers and pinks. Use sparingly to flavour jellies, fruit compotes, stewed fruits and fresh fruit salads.

herbal sauces

Sauces, herbal or otherwise, have a long-standing and (unfortunately) well-earned reputation for being 'bad' – not in terms of flavour, for they can turn an ordinary recipe into a delight, but in terms of health. Overflowing with calories, oozing with butter and running with rivers of cream, the old-fashioned high-fat, high-cholesterol recipes enjoyed by the last generation were almost as bad for your heart as the greasy-spoon fry-up.

But to rewrite the old proverb, 'eating a dish without sauce is like kissing a man without a beard'. Yes, there is a bit of cholesterol here and there, as well as a little saturated fat from the occasional dollop of cream or the odd knob of butter. Mostly, however, these sauces are made with low-fat crème fraîche, fromage frais, yoghurt and olive oil. The key constituents are the herbs that so readily give up their flavour and health-giving properties. Listed below are just a few ideas for some wonderful sauces, yet they're not the gospel according to St Michael: there are no rules here, so follow your instincts and your taste buds and be a brave experimenter.

Spanish garlic sauce
Extracted with great linguistic difficulty from 'María', a wonderful cook at a street-side *venta* in Frigiliana, southern Spain, this sauce makes a delicious complement to any firm, cooked vegetables. It will breathe new life into broccoli, courgettes, cauliflower, runner and broad beans – and yes, even the most traditional Brussels sprouts.

1 Place two cloves of garlic, a handful each of celery leaves and parsley, and six mint leaves into a liquidizer or blender with a tablespoon or two of water and whizz to a purée.

2 Add a tablespoon of cider vinegar to enough water to cover a thick slice of bread, without crusts.

3 When thoroughly soaked, pour off the liquid and squeeze the bread.

4 Add to the liquidizer and slowly add six tablespoons of olive oil.

5 Season with black pepper and pour over vegetables. If the sauce is too thick, simply beat in a little water.

Pumpkin sauce

This unusual sauce goes well with goose and duck and livens up an everyday chicken.

1 Cook 450 g (1 lb) of pumpkin pieces until tender.

2 Put the pieces in a food processor along with a couple of tinned tomatoes, a clove of garlic, a pinch of cinnamon and a teaspoon of rosemary leaves.

3 Add a generous tablespoon of rosemary vinegar and some of the pumpkin cooking water. Whiz until smooth.

Sinful sorrel purée

This recipe contains cream and butter, but the nutritional and cleansing properties of sorrel offset the indulgence. For variations on the theme, use rocket or spinach. This one is great with poached eggs and delicious with white fish, pork or rabbit.

1 Sweat a handful of washed, chopped sorrel leaves in a small knob of butter, stirring constantly, for about three minutes.

2 Add a tablespoon of chopped flat-leafed parsley, a pinch of nutmeg and four tablespoons of single cream.

Simple apple sauce

An apple a day may keep the doctor away, but everyone really needs two for the maximum cholesterol and blood-pressure lowering benefits. Add the protective, mood-enhancing properties of sage to this quick and easy sauce. As a variation, substitute mint for the sage. This one is delicious with hot or cold meats and poultry.

1 Finely chop four red or purple sage leaves.

2 Peel, core and slice two large cooking apples.

3 Place apples, sage and a dessertspoon of runny honey into a saucepan with the minimum amount of water.

4 Cook slowly over a low heat until mushy.

All-heal herb sauce

A genuine supersauce: antiseptic, antifungal, antiviral, good for the urinary system and heart and loaded with vitamin C. It improves if kept for a day or two (covered) in the fridge. Use on all salads, fish and grills.

1 Put six tablespoons of olive oil, two tablespoons of any herb vinegar, four tablespoons of lemon juice, two teaspoons of runny honey, four to six spring onion bulbs (depending on size), one tablespoon of flat-leafed parsley and a generous addition of fresh thyme, tarragon and marjoram in a food processor.

2 Process until finely chopped and smooth.

a prac

herbs

tical

guide

growing herbs

If, like many people, you're rediscovering the taste and health benefits of all these wonderful herbs, you can enhance the joys of cooking and derive enormous satisfaction by growing your own. Growing your own herbs is not only easy but time saving, convenient and very cost effective. Compare the price of a few sprigs of fresh sage, thyme or basil in a plastic packet in the supermarket with the cost of a whole packet of seeds, and you'll see what I mean!

Plant for convenience

If you have a garden, don't make the mistake of planting your herbs at the very end of the vegetable plot; they need to be as close to the kitchen door as possible so that you can nip out and snip a few leaves the instant you need them. Planting your herbs in a convenient spot also means that you get the fullest flavour and maximum medicinal benefit from the volatile oils and other active constituents, which start to degrade as soon as the herbs are harvested.

If you don't have a garden or a suitable cultivated area near the kitchen, most culinary herbs can be successfully grown in various sizes of pots, tubs, window-boxes and other suitable containers.

Situation and depth

Whichever method you choose, most herbs prefer light, well-drained soil and plenty of sun – but there are exceptions. Horseradish, for example, needs rich, deep soil; mint, which is happier with damp roots, can be very invasive and take over the rest of your herb patch. These two should be grown in a separate area: an old bucket with the bottom knocked out will contain the spread of the mints and horseradish.

If circumstances dictate that you can only use pots and containers, then most herbs are happy

with a depth of about 30 cm (12 inches).
The smaller herbs will thrive happily in
window-boxes at a depth of around 20 cm
(eight inches). Naturally large plants like bay trees,
and the shrubby bushes of sage and rosemary will
thrive in much larger pots.

For container growing, good drainage is essential and drainage
holes need to be covered with plenty of broken pot shards or fine wire mesh.
Containers should not stand directly on the ground but should be raised on stones,
pieces of pot or tile or the easily available terracotta feet. This encourages drainage in
the summertime and prevents waterlogging and frost damage in the winter.

Creative containers

Be imaginative with your containers. I've used old stone jars, cast-iron water troughs, old watering
cans… even a couple of galvanised zinc troughs discarded by plasterers and the drum of an old concrete
mixer. As long as you drill sufficient drainage holes, anything that has an interesting shape will make a
good addition to the herb garden.

The right compost

There are many ready-made container composts available from garden centres, but I've found the
very best of the growing mediums is that recommended by Jekka McVicar, the leading British herb
grower and frequent winner of medals at the Chelsea Flower Show. (For information on growing every
conceivable culinary herb, see her *Complete Herb Book*, details of which are listed in 'sources', page
138.) Jekka recommends a mixture of equal parts of bark, peat (or peat substitute) and grit, which she
says prevents over-watering and under-watering and helps the compost absorb water more efficiently
if it does dry out. She recommends it for both containers and hanging baskets – another good place to
grow your herbs.

Containers and baskets will all need regular watering and feeding, and you will need to renew the
compost completely every four or five years in the bigger containers. Shallow window-boxes and small pots
will need changing annually. Make sure that you consider the final height of the plant before choosing its
pot so that the taller varieties don't become unstable and fall over.

Creating a herb garden

There are many gardening books that provide detailed instructions on laying out a herb garden. Depending on space, time and money, you can create anything from a tiny corner filled with half a dozen of your kitchen favourites to a classic walled herb garden, a knot garden or even a traditional formal parterre. If you run out of space in the borders, then remember that all the sages, rosemary, parsley, scented geraniums and borage do well in large pots, while clumps of small herbs such as thyme, oregano, tarragon, marjoram, savory and wild strawberry look beautiful in traditional strawberry pots which have openings around the side as well as in the top.

In fact, virtually all the herbs you'll want can be grown in containers, but although you can buy many of them as plants in specialist nurseries and garden centres, some will have to be grown from seed. Annuals and biennials – basil, borage, dill, fennel, parsley, summer and winter savory, and so on – are all best propagated yourself; most can be sown between April and May. The less hardy herbs should not be sown until all danger of frost has passed.

Flower power

Don't forget that the flowers of many herbs are both beneficial and delicious, so make sure they're easy to get to when you plan your garden or the layout of your containers. Garlic, chives, lavender, sage, hyssop, camomile, rocket, nasturtiums and pinks are some of the most popular to bear in mind.

The herbal year

Spring is the time to re-pot your herbs if the roots show signs of coming through the bottom of the pot.

During the summer, keep plants dead-headed and remember that even if it rains, little water will get into the pot and most will still need watering every day.

In autumn, the perennials need cutting back quite hard to stop them getting 'leggy', while in winter, even the hardy pot plants will need protection from very severe weather. Covering them with horticultural fleece not only protects the plants but the pots, too. This is a necessary precaution, as I've found to my cost, as even the most expensive terracotta pots that are supposed to withstand frost may crack if the weather gets very cold.

If it's at all possible, give your containers extra protection by putting them under cover for the worst of the winter; even the garage is better than nothing. Water very occasionally, using the absolute minimum needed to keep the soil from drying out completely.

Recipes: fresh versus dried

When using your fresh herbs, remember that they are much less strongly flavoured than their dried counterparts, so be sparing in the amounts of dried herbs you add to recipes. As a general rule, remember that a teaspoonful of any dried leaf produces the same flavour intensity as a tablespoon of the fresh chopped plant.

Companion planting

Besides their obvious culinary benefits, herbs make a useful addition to any garden – particularly as many make ideal companion plants that help control weeds and other pests. Set them as close as possible to the other plants you wish to protect, and you'll be making a good start towards some useful – and organic – pest control.

Chives, for example, and other members of the onion family, help keep aphids away from susceptible ornamental plants such as roses (although if you have a lettuce crop, chives also seem to keep visiting rabbits away). Similarly, planting garlic near rose bushes is said to deter black spot. Planting summer savory alongside bean crops will help reduce blackfly populations, while rosemary repels such unwanted 'guests' as the cabbage caterpillar and the carrot fly.

Aromatic and flowering herbs also benefit the garden in other ways. Hyssop, sage, savory and thyme, for example, attract bees and butterflies, which then pollinate your other plants; they also appeal to hoverflies, whose larvae feed on aphids and other garden pests.

Other 'herbal guardians' include dill, which is repellent to spider mites; scented geraniums, which help deter leafhoppers; pennyroyal, which repels aphids; and southernwood, which is apparently avoided by ants, aphids, cabbage moths and flea beetles. Mint is also good at repelling everything from cabbage caterpillars to mice, but as it's highly invasive, remember to keep it confined to a pot.

harvesting and drying

Although the flavours of herbs are best when they are harvested straight from the growing plant, it's simple to dry them for use during periods when fresh plants may not be available. So long as you are prepared to take sufficient care and trouble, your own home-dried herbs will be infinitely superior to any of the commercially available dried products. With a little effort, is not difficult to have a wide selection of valuable dried culinary herbs that will have a richer, fuller flavour and better aroma than their shop-bought equivalents. And, if you've grown them organically, you'll know that they've never been exposed to dangerous agrochemicals.

What to dry?

Some of the best herbs for drying are dill, tarragon, bay, oregano, rosemary, sage, and thyme. Fennel and coriander are also great dried for their seeds, and you can easily dry juniper berries. Besides ensuring a constant supply of herbs, drying also helps the amount of fresh herbs you'll get; in general, the more you cut from your herb plants, the more vigorous their growth becomes. As well as your regular daily use of herbs, you should be able to make two collections for drying during each season.

When and how to harvest

The highest concentration of aroma and flavour is present just before flowering, so this is the time to harvest your herbs for long-term storage. To avoid bruising and loss of flavour, make sure you harvest with a very sharp knife or pair of scissors. It's much better to use three-inch sprigs rather than removing individual leaves, and to keep plants looking good, collect your cuttings from all over the plant to maintain an attractive shape.

Collect herbs for drying early on during a sunny morning. The perfect moment is just after the dew has evaporated and before the sun's heat draws out the volatile oils, yet gathering on a cloudy day is fine as long as there is no humidity.

After harvesting, lay your herbs in a flat, shallow basket, as piling them on top of each other will lead to bruising and loss of flavour. If the herbs need cleaning, just dip them in cold water and dry quickly and gently with soft kitchen paper.

The drying process

Optimum flavour is retained only by rapid drying, which needs plenty of circulating air and only moderate heat. In order to ensure that your dried herbs retain as much colour as possible, they should be kept away from direct sunlight.

Individual herbs need slightly different temperatures and times for drying, and these can also vary according to the condition of the plant when harvesting, and to prevailing ambient temperature and humidity. Generally speaking, temperatures between 21°C (70°F) and 38°C (100°F) will cover most requirements. This can be achieved in an airing cupboard with the door left slightly ajar, a loft space which is warm but dark (cover any skylight windows), or in an oven at very low temperatures with the door ajar.

If you have a weatherproof garden shed with covered windows and a gentle heat source, you could also use it for herb drying. Don't, however, hang bunches in your garage, as the drying plants can readily absorb the unpleasant aromas of petrol, diesel fuel and exhaust fumes.

Separate and circulate

Keep different varieties separate in order to avoid flavour contamination, and lay the herbs on a muslin-covered rack (turn two or three times a day for the first 48 hours), or hang them in small bunches. Seeds may be collected by tying a paper bag over the flower heads and hanging from the stems till the seeds have dropped; do not use plastic bags as they sweat. Once collected, seeds need to be laid out for drying, which may take another ten to 14 days.

If drying your herbs in a loft, or even in the spare room with the curtains drawn, a small fan will help maintain good air circulation, which speeds up the drying process and prevents the growth of any mould.

It's easy to tell when your herbs are sufficiently dry as the leaves become brittle and break easily into small pieces. Remove the leaves from thick stems and rub them into small pieces. Take care not to overdo this process – otherwise you'll end up with herb powder.

Microwave techniques

It is possible to use a microwave for really rapid herb drying – though not possessing one myself, I've never tried. Herb grower Jekka McVicar (*see* 'sources' on page 138) says that she dries small-leafed herbs such as rosemary and thyme in about a minute, while larger leaves like mint take about three. She advises adding an eggcup-ful of water to the microwave and warns that it's easy to cook and destroy the leaves if you leave them in too long.

storing and freezing

Thanks to modern technology, the pleasures of growing and using herbs can be extended throughout the year by employing the simple methods of storing and freezing plants directly from the garden, patio, balcony or window-box.

Storing dried herbs

Once you've gone to all the trouble of drying your herbs, it is vital to be sure that you store them properly. Place dried herbs and seeds in air-tight, screw-top, preferably dark, glass jars, and keep them in a dry cupboard or pantry. If dried herbs are exposed to moisture and sunlight, they will quickly lose their quality, and all your hard work will have been for nothing. Don't be tempted to use plastic containers as they tend to sweat, which encourages mildew. If well dried and properly stored, your herbs should keep their flavours for up to 18 months.

Pick of the bunch

We've all been tempted by the decorative quality of bunches of herbs hanging from the kitchen ceiling. Be warned: herbs dried and/or stored in this way are likely to be swamped by other kitchen odours and will be exposed to more moisture and light than is good for them. If you must hang bunches do so in the proper surroundings as mentioned on page 104 – or keep them in the kitchen for decoration only!

The frozen alternative

If the drying process sounds like too much effort, then don't lose heart: freezing is another wonderful way of storing some herbs for later use. One of the benefits of freezing is that you preserve the plants' vivid colours as well as their flavours – although their general appearance will be such that you'll probably want to reserve frozen herbs for sauces, stews and soups.

The process of freezing is quick and easy and there's no need for blanching. It's important to wrap all herbs in plastic bags before placing them in the freezer, as their strong aromas can easily contaminate any other foods that may be stored there.

Once individual bags are frozen, they can be then be stored in freezer containers. This method provides double protection against contamination as well as protection from the physical damage caused by 'freezer burn'.

Don't forget to label the containers, however, as otherwise you might just end up ruining a recipe! Once frozen, most herbs should keep their flavours well for up to six months.

What to freeze?

Herbs that freeze brilliantly include chives, chervil, coriander, lemon balm, all the mints, basils, parsley, sweet cicely, sorrel, savory (winter and summer) and tarragon.

Using frozen herbs

One big advantage of using the freezer to store your herbs is that there is no need to thaw them before utilizing them in recipes. In fact, this would be a decided disadvantage, as it then becomes impossible to chop them properly.

Parsley, for example, should be taken from the freezer, then crushed while still in its bag and brittle; once that has been done, you can then sprinkle it easily onto the appropriate dish. The same method can be used for most frozen herbs.

Cube it!

One of my favourite methods of freezing herbs – and one that is even easier than using plastic bags – is to freeze some of them, finely chopped, into ice-cubes.

Chop up enough of the fresh herbs, such as parsley, chives or tarragon, to be able to place a couple of teaspoons of each into an individual ice-cube compartment; then fill with water and freeze. When the cubes are solid, you can empty them into labelled bags or containers and just take out a few at a time to add directly to recipes.

Again, there's no need to thaw, and these herbal cubes are great to have on hand when you need to prepare a quick meal at short notice.

ng
herbs

the
phar

herbal
macy

herbs that

If you wake up with a sore throat, do you dash to the doctor for antibiotics? If indigestion strikes, do you reach for antacids? Attacked by a flu virus, do you opt for packets of patent medicines? When arthritis flares, are you forced to choose between pain relief or an upset stomach triggered by anti-inflammatory drugs?

Many people aren't aware that herbs can help to prevent and treat these and many other day-to-day ailments. From minor and trivial discomforts to life-threatening diseases, using the right herbs in your daily cooking can – and will – enhance your quality of life by protecting you, mentally and physically, from the ravages of Western civilization. In many instances, these natural alternatives can replace other forms of medication. Even in more serious conditions, they can allow you to reduce the amount of conventional drugs you're taking – with, of course, the knowledge and approval of your physician.

High blood pressure, joint disease, chronic digestive problems, irritable bowel syndrome, raised cholesterol levels, skin disorders and even asthma can be eased by some of the everyday herbs you might already use in cooking. Yet herbs alone cannot reverse an unhealthy lifestyle. There's little point in using garlic to lower your cholesterol, for example, if you only eat it in a dish oozing with saturated fat. Similarly, irritable bowel syndrome won't respond to anise, fennel, marshmallow and mint – all good for digestive problems – if you live on a diet of burgers and chips, packets of biscuits, white bread and salted peanuts.

heal

If you want to incorporate the benefits of herbs into a healthy lifestyle, however, then look no further. This herbal pharmacy explains which medicinal benefits are offered by each of the 65 culinary herbs, what they're good for and how to use them. Whether it's leaves, flowers, stems or roots, in soups or sauces, whether they are used with meat, fish, poultry or in desserts, you'll find all the information you need. If you'd rather not spend much time in the kitchen, take heart: many of these plants make excellent teas, so you can enjoy their medicinal properties by making some (mainly) pleasant alternatives to conventional tea or coffee.

Do be adventurous and try some of the more unusual herbs, as all those listed have health benefits as well as delicious and sometimes unusual flavours. Everyone knows that horseradish makes your eyes water, for example, but you may not know that it is also a powerful antibacterial, an expectorant and a circulatory stimulant – which means that it's good for treating colds, fevers, flu, chest infections and chilblains. It isn't common knowledge, either, that hyssop can help asthmatics, juniper is good for gout and cystitis, or that lady's mantle is an ancient remedy for painful periods. Besides having a wonderful flavour, lemon verbena tea functions as an antidepressant; besides pleasing the eye, marigold petals make a powerful detoxifier. All these plants, and many others, appear in the recipes that make up the rest of this book. What better way to take your natural 'medicine'?

herb	source of	good for	how to use
Angelica	Limonene, borneol, phthalates, xanthotoxol (an anti-nicotinic) and angelicin	Digestive problems and increasing peripheral circulation. A good cleansing and aphrodisiac herb.	Add chopped leaves to cooked fruit or drinks; their natural sweetness reduces the need for sugar.
Anise	The volatile oil estragole, anisic acid, carvone and dianethole, which has oestrogenic properties	Increasing sexual drive and milk production during breast-feeding. Also reduces wind and colic and helps with period pains, asthma and bronchitis.	Add ground seeds or fresh chopped leaves to fish, salads, vegetables or soups.
Basil	Linalool, estragole, borneol, eugenol, beta-carotene and some vitamin C	Cleansing, mood-enhancing and as an antibacterial. Useful in all kidney and urinary problems.	Add leaves to salads, soups, poultry and particularly pasta and cheese dishes. Also excellent in herb vinegar or oil (see page 94).
Bay	Cineole, linalool, limonene and laurenolide	Upper respiratory infections, the relief of joint pain and indigestion. Also useful in bringing on delayed periods and as a powerful mood-enhancer. A cleansing and energising herb.	In soups, stews, casseroles and marinades. Also surprisingly good infused in milk-based puddings. The best flavour is from fresh leaves, though dried are widely available and you can also buy ground bay powder.
Bergamot	Thymol, a powerful antiseptic	Protection against infections, especially colds and bronchitis. Also useful as a tonic for new mothers, and to help increase libido and regulate periods.	As tea made from chopped leaves. Flowers can be added to salads and cold, savoury dishes, while fresh chopped leaves can be added to salad dressings.

herb	source of	good for	how to use
Borage	Pyrrolizidine alkaloids, amabaline and supinine; also contains soothing mucilage and antiseptic tannins	Relief of respiratory discomfort and diuretic effects. Seeds very rich in omega-3 fatty acids, so it is also good for eczema and other skin problems, and menstrual disorders.	With caution. Excessive quantities over long periods can be toxic, but borage's delicious finely chopped leaves can be added to yoghurt, fromage frais, goats cheese or salad. Use whole leaves in Pimms or any chilled fruit drinks, and flowers to make an excellent garnish for any dish.
Capers	Capric acid	Constipation, strengthening capillaries and boosting circulation.	Normally pickled in vinegar. Rinsed, they make a good addition to sauces for fish and lamb, and give extra flavour to salads, pasta and egg dishes.
Caraway	Flavonoids, polysaccharides and carvone	Cleansing, relaxing intestinal muscles for the relief of colic, pain, bloating, flatulence and abdominal cramp. Also used as an expectorant for chest infections.	The distinctive flavour of seeds is good in soups, cheeses and vegetables such as cabbage, Brussels sprouts, etc. Use the milder leaves in salads, sauces and marinades.
Catmint (also called Catnip or Catnep)	Iridoids, tannins and geraniol	Upset stomachs, reducing fever. Excellent as tea for children with colds or flu, and it is cleansing and mood-enhancing.	Use leaves in sauces or infusions, leaves and flowers in salads, leaves and young shoots with mixed herbs for poultry, lamb and game.
Camomile	Chamazulene, flavonoids and phenolic acids	Reducing temperatures, especially in children, nausea, poor appetite, insomnia, migraine. Protects against infections, and is also mood-enhancing.	Not widely used in food, but hugely valuable as an infusion, both internally and externally. It also makes an excellent rinse for fair hair.

herb	source of	good for	how to use
Chervil	Coumarins, flavonoids and volatile oil	Cleansing and protection. Also helps purify blood, aids digestion, is diuretic and helps reduce high blood pressure.	A traditional component of French *fines herbes*, chervil's delicate parsley-like flavour with a hint of aniseed is best added just before serving. It goes with many foods, especially eggs.
Chicory	Coumarins, chicoriin, umbelliferone and scopoletin	Use as a cleansing and power herb, a diuretic and as a tonic for the liver and gall bladder. It is also helpful for gout and rheumatism.	Tender leaves and flowers can be added to salads or infused as tea. The dried, ground root makes a coffee substitute.
Chives	Contains sulphurous substances, including allicin, flavonoids and phenolic acid	Reducing cholesterol and blood pressure, also as an antibiotic and antifungal.	The gentlest-flavoured of the onion family, chives make wonderful sauces and butter. They combine with virtually everything from eggs, cheese and salad to meat and potatoes. The flowers look and taste wonderful; float them on soup or add to salads.
Coriander	Linalool, alpha-pinene, coriandrol, angelicin and psoralen	Cleansing, mood-enhancing and aphrodisiac properties. Also effective against indigestion and colic.	The leaves and seeds are both valuable, but very different. Unripe seeds smell awful – don't use them. The flavour improves with storage after gathering. The pungent, slightly peppery taste of the leaves goes wonderfully with salads, sauces, soups and fish. Use crushed leaves in stews, casseroles or hamburgers.
Cowslip	Tannins, many anti-inflammatory flavonoids, saponins, phenols and primulic acid	Both leaves and flowers have cleansing and protective qualities. The plant is also weakly diuretic and mildly sedative. The flowers are good for hyperactive and insomniac children.	Add leaves and flowers to salads. Use flowers to make cowslip wine.

herb	source of	good for	how to use
Curry plant	Nerol, sesquiterpenes and flavonoids	Use as a very mild expectorant.	The curry plant's mild flavour is best added towards the end of cooking. It is especially good in salads or with poultry and eggs. Use leaves or sprigs.
Dandelion	Carotenoids (including lutein), potassium, vitamin C, taraxacoside, taraxerol	This cleansing and power herb is a strong diuretic, tonic and anti-inflammatory. There's even some evidence of anti-tumour benefits. Good for kidney and liver problems, also rheumatism.	The slightly bitter young leaves are delicious in salads. Sold on every street market in France as *pis en lit* ('wet the bed') but difficult to find in UK shops. If you're growing it to eat, keep cats and dogs away.
Dill	Carvone, eugenol, myristicin, xanthones	Cleansing and mood-enhancing. Excellent for colic in babies, digestive problems and IBS in adults. Increases mothers' milk production and helps relieve menstrual pain.	Sprinkle leaves on fish, particularly in marinades and pickling. Seeds and leaves are good with vegetables. Makes a good herb vinegar (*see* page 95).
Elder	Flowers contain rutin, tannins, triterpenes and essential fatty acids. Berries are rich in vitamins A and C and strongly protective anthocyanins	Use as a strongly protective herb. Also acts as an anti-inflammatory, helps all catarrhal problems, arthritis and gout. Berries boost the immune system.	Use flowers for infusions or add to dessert dishes. Berries should be used cooked only as preserves or with other fruit, particularly apples.
Evening primrose	Essential linolenic and gamma-linolenic oils	PMS, breast pain, eczema and dry skin. A protective and power herb, new evidence suggests the evening primrose may help hyperactivity and dyslexia.	Mostly as oil extracted from seeds, but leaves and flowerbuds are edible.

herb	source of	good for	how to use
Fennel	Anethole, fenchone	Wind and colic in children. It is also mildly diuretic and helps regulate hormone balance in women.	Infuse seeds for drinking and as compresses, especially for dry, itchy eyes. The seeds and leaves are excellent with fish, lamb and offal. Delicious in vinegar and oil.
Garlic	Sulphur compounds allicin and alliin, the enzyme allinace and selenium	High blood pressure and cholesterol, chest infections, fungal infections, digestion – and almost everything else that might ail you.	Best eaten raw. Chop and let stand for ten minutes before cooking. Makes excellent oils and vinegars and can be used in everything from soups to ice-cream.
Feverfew	Pinene, parthenolide, chrysanthemonin	Headaches, migraine, arthritis, rheumatism. As a general anti-inflammatory, it is good for most pains.	Two to three leaves daily may help prevent migraine attacks, but eat in a sandwich to avoid mouth ulcers from this bitter, astringent herb. Add one or two finely shredded leaves to salads.
Honeysuckle	Salicylic acid and tannins	Use as a mild laxative and expectorant. May help reduce severity of asthma and inflammatory bowel disease.	Add flowers to salads or use to make infusions – either to drink or as cold compresses for itchy skin.
Hops	Valerianic acid, humulene and oestrogenic substances	Insomnia, anxiety, stress, indigestion and muscle spasm.	Make infusions of dried herb into tea. Add leaves to soups. A bowl of dried flowers in the bedroom is calming and mood-enhancing.
Horseradish	Sinigrin; when crushed, this turns into the anti-bacterial allyl isothiocyanate. Also some vitamin C	Promotes sweating and is a good diuretic; useful in fevers, colds and flu, also as an expectorant. Its antibacterial properties help all types of infection. General digestive and circulatory stimulant and a powerful nasal decongestant.	The root may be grated as a condiment. Also add to dips and sauces. As a poultice, it relieves chilblains.

herb	source of	good for	how to use
Hyssop	Terpenes, camphor, flavonoids and the expectorant marubiin	Stimulation and calming. It's also valuable for coughs, bronchitis and asthma, and is soothing for burns.	Add leaves and flowers to salads. Add leaves to stews and casseroles; they help with the digestion of fat. A weak tea made from the flowers can be applied as a compress to burns.
Juniper	Volatile oils pinene, limonene, tannins and many other substances with antibacterial properties	The relief of cystitis, gout, osteoarthritis and rheumatism. It is also diuretic and anti-inflammatory, and good for catarrh.	The crushed berries make a wonderful addition to game birds, marinades and casseroles, especially venison. Pour boiling water over the berries for catarrh-relieving inhalations.
Lady's mantle	Tannins, glycosides and salicylic acid	Menstrual pain and irregularity. Also helpful for diarrhoea.	Add the bright green leaves to salads or use them to make tea for menstrual problems or fibroids.
Lavender	More than 40 phytochemicals, including flavonoids, tannins and coumarins; also a high percentage of volatile oils	Use as an anti-inflammatory, so it is good for arthritis, toothache and headaches. Helpful for treatment of asthma, indigestion, wind, insomnia and migraine.	Add flowers and leaves to ice-cream, biscuits and preserves. Make tea from one teaspoon of dried or two teaspoons of fresh flowers (removed from the stalk) to a cup of boiling water.
Lemon balm (also known as Balm Melissa and Cure All)	Citronella, linalool, polyphenols and tannins	Use as a good digestive, relaxant and headache cure. Traditionally used as a heart tonic and antidepressant. New research shows that the polyphenols are antiviral and protect against cold sores caused by the herpes simplex virus.	Use the leaves chopped and sprinkled over fish or salads, to make tea for relief of headaches and stress or added to vinegar for their fresh flavour and health-giving properties. Add them to cheese-based dips.

herb	source of	good for	How to use
Lemon verbena	Limonene, geraniole, citral, mucilage and flavonoids	Use as a gentle sedative, also for digestive problems. It is also a useful antidepressant.	Use the leaves to make a refreshing, soothing infusion: one teaspoon dried or two teaspoons fresh leaves to a cup of boiling water. They can also be added to ice-cream and to cooked fruit desserts.
Lovage	Extremely rich in volatile oils, especially phthalids, terpenes, coumarins and psoralen	Diuretic action, exceptionally good for the relief of wind; also stimulates the appetite, relieves period pains and makes a natural deodoriser.	In soup, like sorrel and rocket. Add to salads or cook like spinach. Put a sprig in the kids' smelly trainers and a cup of lovage tea in your bath for natural freshness.
Marigold	Carotenes, flavonoids, volatile oils and bitter glycosides	Use as an antiseptic and antifungal. Also good for gastritis, colitis and as a powerful detoxifier for the skin and liver. Can be helpful for acne and eczema, and helps control irregular periods.	Make tea from fresh or dried flowers and use for digestive, liver, skin and menstrual problems. Tea can also be applied externally for fungal infections like athletes' foot, ringworm or thrush. Use the flower petals in cake or bread recipes, or add them to scrambled eggs. Young, tender leaves can be torn and added to salads.
Marjoram (*Oreganum majorana* or Sweet Marjoram; related to Oregano, *see* page 122)	Sabinene, linalool, carvacrol, estrogole and eugenol	Use as a protective, energising and cleansing herb; also as an antiviral, antioxidant and aid to digestion.	This is the strongest flavoured of the marjorams, and it is ideal for herb vinegars, meat sauces, casseroles, oily fish, stuffings and pasta.

herb	source of	good for	how to use
Marshmallow	Starch, soothing mucilage and the soluble fibre pectin. Also contains tannins, asparagine and glucan	Soothing inflammation of the digestive tract and mucous membranes; also as an effective antacid, gentle laxative and anti-inflammatory, so it is effective for all inflammatory bowel diseases. Strongly protective.	The roots, leaves and flowers are all edible. Leaves and flowers make good oils and vinegars. Roots can be boiled and eaten as vegetables.
Mint	There are many varieties of mint, with slightly varying compositions, but very different flavours, ranging from apple to ginger. The constituents most common to all types are menthol, menthone and menthyl acetate	All digestive problems, most particularly indigestion. Also functions as a protective and mood-enhancing herb, which, when applied to the skin relieves migraine and other headaches.	The leaves are traditionally used in potato and vegetable cooking water. Mint sauce and jelly are common accompaniments to lamb. Torn leaves make an excellent addition to salad. Also good with fruit, particularly apples and gooseberries, sorbets and other desserts (especially with chocolate), drinks and particularly as mint tea. Makes delicious vinegar.
Myrtle	Myrtenol, pyrogallols, tannins and flavonoids	Urinary infections and digestive problems. Also highly protective and a traditional aphrodisiac.	Make tea from the leaves, which have a spicy flavour. Leaves can be added to barbecued and grilled meats. Grind dried berries and use with game, especially venison, quail and partridge.
Nasturtium	Myrosin, spilanthol, glucocyanates and oxalic acid	Antibacterial action and immune-boosting; also for use as an aphrodisiac herb. Enhanced immunity comes from the vitamin C content of the leaves and flowers.	The sharp, peppery flavour of the leaves goes well in salads or in unusual sandwiches. The flowers, which you can now buy in some supermarkets, are a most attractive and edible garnish. **Note:** Don't eat leaves if you have gout.

herb	source of	good for	how to use
Nettles	Chlorophyll, vitamin C and fibre; also contain histamine, serotonin and useful amounts of potassium and calcium	Protection and power. Nettles are also diuretic, detoxifying and, as tea, are helpful for arthritis, eczema and fluid retention. Because of its histamine content, the tea is also helpful for asthma, hay fever and skin allergies.	Make a wonderfully nutritious soup. Also use as a tea: add two teaspoons of freshly chopped leaves to a cup of boiling water.
Oregano (*Oreganum vulgare* or Wild Marjoram)	Thymol, bisabolene, caryophyllene, linalool and borneol	Strong protection, mood-enhancing and reputedly aphrodisiac, with antiviral and antibacterial properties.	Perfect with tomatoes and all tomato-based foods. Delicious sprinkled on lamb, chicken and delicate fish – and a pizza isn't Italian without it.
Parsley	Volatile oils, including apiole, eugenol, limonene, myristicin; also flavonoids, including apigenin. Rich in carotenoids, vitamin C and iron	Use as a strong diuretic, expectorant, anti-inflammatory and a powerful antioxidant. A cleansing and mood-enhancing herb with a medicinal history stretching back to ancient Greece and Rome.	French broad-leaf parsley has a slightly stronger flavour, but is more pleasant to eat than the curly variety. A major constituent of *bouquet garni*, which enhances the flavours of most savoury dishes, it is very widely used as a garnish, but don't leave it on the side of your plate; it's nutritionally much too valuable to waste. Use the leaves, coarsely chopped, to make a diuretic tea.
Pennyroyal (*Mentha pulegium*)	Volatile oil: mostly pulegone, with some menthol, limonene, bitters and tannins	Digestive problems, particularly flatulence. As a weak infusion, pennyroyal is good for colds and is a traditional treatment for bringing on delayed periods.	This herb has a very strong peppermint flavour, so use it sparingly but exactly like other mints. Its name comes from *pulga* (Latin for 'flea'); tied in muslin bags, it makes an excellent natural flea repellent.

herb	source of	good for	how to use
Pinks	Eugenol and salicylates	This mood-enhancing power-flower is used in traditional Chinese medicine for urinary infections and by European herbalists to treat anxiety and heart conditions.	Pull the petals from the flowers and remove their bitter white tips. Petals add delicious flavour to cooked fruits, jams and jellies, or may be used in oils and vinegars. Steeped in sweet white wine, they make an effective, delicious and enjoyable tonic.
Primrose	Primulaveroside, glycosides and flavonoids	Rheumatic and arthritic conditions, as this protective and cleansing plant is a natural anti-inflammatory. It is a also gentle sedative and is useful in treating chest infections.	Cook primrose leaves like spinach and mix with a little extra-virgin olive oil and nutmeg. The flowers made a wonderful edible decoration in salads.
Purslane	Mucilage, vitamins, calcium. Most importantly, it is one of the few vegetable sources of omega-3 essential fatty acids	Gentle diuretic, anti-diarrhoeal and antibacterial properties. It is also a protective, cleansing and aphrodiasic herb.	Add to salads as they do in Morocco, Iran and most of the Middle East. Purslane is rarely seen in the UK, but has been used widely as food and medicine since Roman times.
Rocket	Tannins, salicylates and the volatile oils saffronal, cinelle and crocins	Cleansing, as a mild expectorant and as an analgesic.	Add the leaves to any salad for their distinctive peppery flavour. It is also good as soup, or served in pasta and sauces. Rocket was used as food and medicine in Elizabethan times.
Rose	Hips: huge amounts of vitamin C, carotenoids, B vitamins, pectin, tannins, citronellol, geraniol and nerol. Petals: similar to above, but in smaller amounts	Mood-enhancing and aphrodisiac properties. Extract of hips, infusions of petals and rosewater function as anti-diarrhoeal, immune-boosting, cholesterol-reducing and antidepressant substances.	Rose-hip jelly or syrup and rosewater can all be added to desserts. Rose petals may be used as edible decorations in salads and sweet dishes.

herb	source of	good for	how to use
Rosemary	Rosmarinic acid, rosmaricine, flavonoids and volatile oils which include linalool, camphor and borneol	This energising, aphrodisiac, cleansing and mood-enhancing herb has wide-ranging medicinal properties. It is anti-inflammatory, stimulating, analgesic and antibacterial, and also protects against capillary fragility.	As an evergreen, rosemary is available fresh throughout the year. Use sprigs for roasting, grilling or on the barbecue or include finely chopped leaves in soups, sauces, salads, pasta or even homemade bread. It also makes wonderful oils and vinegars, is perfect for marinades and, infused as a tea, is a delicious, reviving and beneficial drink.
Saffron	Saffronal, cinelle, crocins, carotenoids and vitamins B_1 and B_2	Aphrodisiac and mood-enhancing, saffron induces menstruation, relieves stomach-ache and wind, and has antidepressant qualities.	Saffron is a traditional colouring for rice, particularly in paella, but it is also good in chicken and lamb casseroles and with fish. Crush with peppercorns, cloves or garlic, then mix with a little water or oil before adding to each dish.
Sage	Thujone, cineole, borneol, salviatannin	There are hundreds of varieties of sage, but purple sage (*Salvia officinalis purpurascens*) has the strongest medicinal action. The widely used Spanish sage, mostly used for cooking, contains no thujone, one of the most important beneficial ingredients. Sage helps balance the female hormone system, is one of the best remedy for sore throats and eases indigestion. This protective, mood-enhancing and power herb should be grown in every garden — even if it's just in a pot on the doorstep.	Because it aids fat digestion, sage is used as a traditional part of stuffing for fatty meats such as port, but it can be added to almost any savoury dish, including omelettes, vegetables, sauces and cooked cheese dishes. Serve as a tea to treat colds and flu.

herb	source of	good for	how to use
Salad burnet	Rutin, tannins and carotenoids	Treating diarrhoea and relieving the discomfort of piles. The protective and cleansing tannins have a mild antiseptic action, so it is also good for infections.	A delightful evergreen garden plant, so you can have fresh leaves all year round to use as a garnish or add early on in the cooking time for stews and casseroles. Salad burnet gives a fresh and different flavour to salads. Make tea from stems, leaves and flowers to treat diarrhoea.
Savory (Summer and Winter)	Volatile oils, which include carvacrol, cymene, linalool and thymol, with phellandrene and limonene. Winter savory contains fewer constituents	Digestion and chest infections, also for a mildly antibacterial action. Summer savory is particularly effective for the prevention and relief of flatulence.	Both varieties have a similar and distinctively pungent flavour. Use with discretion until you've tried it a few times. Good for marinades, salads and strongly flavoured meat. In Europe, summer savory is known as the bean herb due to its ability to prevent the flatulence factor; it is delicious when used with broad beans and all other dried varieties.
Scented geranium	Tannins, geraniin and very small amounts of volatile oil	Digestive disorders, particularly gastric ulcers.	Scented geraniums are used mostly to impart their delicate scent and flavour to sweet dishes, but even here, they are usually infused and discarded before serving. Add to fruit and wine punches, or chop and mix with sorbets, ice-cream and cream for cake toppings.

herb	source of	good for	how to use
Sorrel	Vitamin C, anthaquinones, flavonoids and oxalates	Protection and cleansing. Sorrel is also strongly detoxifying, a diuretic and a gentle laxative. Sheep's sorrel is traditionally used by North American Indians as an anti-cancer treatment.	Sorrel makes wonderful soup and great sauces, particularly for rich meat and poultry such as pork and goose. It can also be added to salads and stuffings, or you can add a few leaves to any vegetables. Note: because of its high oxalic acid content, don't eat sorrel if you have gout or kidney stones.
Southern-wood	Tannins, arbrotannin and strong volatile oils	Use as a general tonic, which also increases digestive efficiency, fights infection and stimulates the appetite. Functions both as a power and cleansing herb.	An infusion can be used for coughs and colds. The strong aromatic leaves can be added in judicious amounts to salads. The flavour combines exceedingly well with sweet desserts – but it can be an acquired taste.
Sweet Cicely	Carotenes, flavonoids, volatile oils and bitter glycosides	Protection and power. Sweet Cicely has been used since the Middle Ages as an energising tonic. The boiled root is traditionally given to sluggish adolescents and senior citizens.	The root, seeds and leaves are edible and sweet, with a hint of anise. Use the leaves to decorate sweet or savoury dishes. Add chopped leaves or pieces of boiled root to salads or to stewing fruit.
Tarragon	Methylchervicol, flavonoids, coumarins and tannins	Protection and mood enhancing. Tarragon is a calming, sleep-inducing herb which also stimulates the flow of gastric juices, thus improving appetite and digestion.	Add tarragon to sauces and stuffings, particularly those served with chicken and fish. It is ideal for oils and vinegars, and also good in spicy drinks such as the Bloody Mary. Infuse leaves as a tea for insomnia.

herb	source of	good for	how to use
Thyme	Thymol, carvacrol, borneol, linalool, geraniol, apigenin and tannins	Use as a strong antiseptic, muscle relaxant, expectorant and antifungal. Highly protective and cleansing, thyme is widely used as an antiseptic mouthwash – the pink liquid by the side of the dentist's chair.	There are many different thymes, but the best for cooking are *Thymus vulgarus* (common garden thyme) and *Thymus citriodorus* (lemon thyme) which go well with practically any savoury recipe. Use orange thyme with duck, silver queen thyme with fish or caraway thyme with beef. Add sprigs to roasts or casseroles and remove before serving, or add leaves alone and discard the stems. Thyme is also good in stuffings, sauces, gravies and with rice, and it makes excellent oils and vinegars.
Welsh onion	(*see* Garlic)	Protection and cleansing. It provides the antiseptic, antibacterial and heart-protective benefits of the onion family.	The leaves are hollow, like thick chives, so use in just the same way. Snip, and add the small circles of leaf to salads, sauces, pasta, stuffings, omelettes, stews and casseroles. The Welsh onion is an ideal plant for small gardens; it will also grow in pots.
Wild strawberry	Fruit: vitamin C, carotenoids, borneol and salicylate. Leaves: tannins and flavonoids	Use as a traditional remedy for menstrual pain and irregularity. Also helpful for diarrhoea.	They're so delicious on their own, it's a waste to do anything else with the tiny fruit. Leaves can be used to make tea. Wild strawberries will grow in window boxes or hanging baskets.
Yarrow	Volatile oils, including pinenes, borneol, eugenol, sabinene, salicylic acid, apigenin, quercetin, artemetin and rutin	Use as a genuine herbal cure-all. Good for fevers, catarrh, colds and high blood pressure. Its anti-inflammatory properties help all rheumatic and arthritic conditions. Yarrow is also useful as a local anaesthetic and can help reduce the risk of blood clots.	Yarrow leaves can be added to salads or used to make a hot tea that is detoxifying, cooling and one of the best herbal remedies for lowering high temperatures. Cold tea can be used on a compress to speed wound healing, prevent infection and also reduce localized pain.

a herbal detox plan

This three-day cleansing plan starts with a short, sharp shock specifically designed to detoxify the liver, rest the kidneys and cleanse the colon. As a bonus, it provides a huge shot in the arm for the body's natural immune defences. Take heed, however: this short fast is not a diet for life, nor is it one that should be followed for weeks on end. Based on the traditional naturopathic principles of fasting, its main objective is to boost the body's protective white-cell count and give it a chance to restore vital functions to their optimum performance.

The detox headache

This plan is pretty low in calories and you will feel hungry from time to time, but don't spoil the effect by cheating. You won't be drinking coffee or ordinary tea, so your caffeine intake will come to an abrupt halt. The combination of less food, no coffee and the effects of detoxification will almost certainly cause a headache. Drink masses of water and try to avoid painkillers. The headache is transient and you are going to feel absolutely great by day four, when you'll be full of all the protective antioxidants you need.

DAY 1
This first detox day is designed to kick-start your metabolism by providing loads of potassium, vitamins B_1, B_6, A, C and E, folic acid and niacin. You should drink at least three pints of fluid – water, weak tea or herbal tea – in addition to the menu below.

Breakfast
One orange, half a grapefruit, and a large slice of melon. One glass of unsalted vegetable juice. One cup of lemon verbena tea, with honey if desired.

Lunch
A plate of raw red and yellow peppers, cucumber, tomato, broccoli, cauliflower, celery, carrots, radishes, fresh parsley and fennel, with extra-virgin olive oil and lemon juice dressing. One large glass of unsweetened fruit juice.

Dinner
A large mixed salad – lettuce, tomato, watercress, onion, garlic, beetroot, celeriac, fresh mint, rocket and thyme – drizzled with extra-virgin olive oil and lemon juice. One large glass of unsweetened fruit juice or unsalted vegetable juice.

DAY 2

The second day of the plan provides an abundance of phosphorus, magnesium, potassium, copper, vitamin B_1, B_6, A, C and E and folic acid, along with protein, calcium, fibre, iron and selenium.

Breakfast
One large glass of hot mint tea with a thick slice of lemon and a tablespoon of honey. One small carton of natural low-fat live yoghurt.

Mid-morning
One large glass of vegetable juice.
One handful each of raisins, dried apricots and fresh nuts

Lunch
A salad of grated carrot, red cabbage, apple, sliced red pepper, tomato, radishes, celery, marjoram, chicory, basil and a sprinkling of sunflower seeds, lemon juice and olive oil. One cup of parsley tea.

Mid-afternoon
A glass of fruit juice and a banana.

Dinner
Any three cooked vegetables (but not potatoes), sprinkled with thyme and capers and drizzled with olive oil, nutmeg and lemon juice. Mint tea.
Evening snack: a mixture of dried fruits and unsalted nuts and as much fresh fruit as you like.

DAY 3

Provides more than the daily requirement of fibre, phosphorus, magnesium, potassium, copper, vitamins B_1, B_2, B_6, A, C and E, niacin, folic acid, along with some vitamin B_{12}, calcium and iron.

Breakfast
A fresh fruit salad of apple, pear, grapes, mango and pineapple. A carton of live yoghurt and a tablespoon of unsweetened muesli. Camomile tea.

Mid-morning
Six dried apricots. A glass of fruit or vegetable juice.

Lunch
Lettuce soup: soften half a chopped onion in a large pan with a little olive oil; add half a shredded Iceberg lettuce, stir for a few minutes, add 900 ml (32 fl oz) of vegetable stock and lots of black pepper; simmer for 20 minutes, then sprinkle with a large handful of chopped parsley. A chunk of crusty wholemeal bread (no butter). Dandelion coffee.

Mid-afternoon
One apple and one pear.

Dinner
Pasta with lettuce pesto: use the rest of the iceberg lettuce from lunch processed with a handful of pine nuts, a little olive oil, one clove of garlic and a carton of low-fat fromage frais. Tomato, onion and yellow pepper salad. Mint tea.

Well done! If you haven't cheated, you're probably four or five pounds lighter, your eyes are bright, your skin is clear and you feel terrific. Powerful herbs have worked their diuretic, cleansing and digestive magic, and all the super-protective natural chemicals in pure, unadulterated food have lifted your spirits, both physically and mentally.

herb yourself better

condition	superherb	effect	how to use
Acne	Dandelion, Fennel, Garlic	Dandelion is both cleansing and diuretic. Fennel stimulates the liver and improves fat digestion. Garlic has antibacterial properties.	Use dandelion leaves in salads. Use fennel as a tea. Use garlic in food.
Anaemia	Chicory, Nettles	Both are good sources of iron.	Use chicory in food, nettles as a tea.
Anxiety	Basil, Camomile, Honeysuckle, Lavender, Rosemary	All have calming effects.	Use camomile in tea, lavender oil in aromatherapy; others may be used in food.
Arthritis	Juniper berries, Marigold, Purslane Wild strawberry	Juniper berries are gently diuretic. Marigold is mildly anti-inflammatory. Purslane is a source of essential fatty acids. Wild strawberry helps excretion of uric acid.	Use juniper berries in food. Use marigold leaves and purslane in salads. Eat the fruit of wild strawberries regularly.
Asthma	Camomile, Nettle	Both improve breathing and relieve congestion.	As teas.
Back pain	Horseradish, Thyme	Horseradish stimulates circulation and helps relieve pain. Thyme serves as a relaxant.	Eat a tsp of freshly grated horseradish in a sandwich. Add thyme to food or to a hot bath.
Boils	Garlic, Marigold, Marjoram, Thyme	Garlic, marjoram and thyme are strong antibacterials. Marigold will draw the boil and soothe painful inflammation.	Use garlic, marjoram and thyme in food; garlic may also be used crushed in a poultice. Use marigold petals to make a hot compress.
Bronchitis	Chives, Coriander, Thyme, Welsh onion	All help relieve congestion. Thyme also makes a useful expectorant.	Use generously in food. Use thyme as a tea: 3 or 4 cups daily.
Bruising	Thyme, Yarrow	Help bruises resolve more quickly.	Take both internally and externally as teas and cold compresses.

condition	superherb	effect	how to use
Catarrh	Elderflower, Garlic, Horseradish, Lavender, Oregano, Nettles, Welsh onion	Elderflower and nettles relieve symptoms when catarrh is allergic in origin. The rest relieve symptoms when infection is involved.	Use elderflower and nettles in recipes and as teas. Use lavender oil in an aromatic burner; place the flowers in a pillow. Use all others in food.
Chilblains	Basil, Chives, Coriander, Sorrel	All help stimulate circulation.	In food.
Cholesterol	Garlic, Chives, Oregano, Purslane	Help eliminate cholesterol.	Eat regularly.
Chronic fatigue	Basil, Bay, Catmint, Lemon Balm, Sage, Southernwood	All help improve mood and generate mental energy, the first step on the road to recovery.	Include in as many recipes as possible.
Circulation problems	Basil, Chives, Coriander, Sorrel	All help stimulate circulation.	Include in as many recipes as possible.
Colds	Chives, Garlic, Elderflower, Peppermint, Welsh Onion, Rosemary, Sage, Thyme, Yarrow	Elderflower and yarrow increase sweating. Chives, garlic and Welsh onion provide antibacterial and mucus-clearing benefits. Rosemary, sage and thyme are all powerful antibacterials and protect the mucous membranes.	Use elderflower and yarrow as teas, chives, garlic and Welsh onion in food. A tsp of equal amounts of mint and yarrow leaves and elderflowers make 1 cup of excellent tea; sweeten with honey and have 3 or 4 cups daily. Rosemary and thyme may be taken in food and as teas. Use sage tea as a gargle. Use essential oils for inhalations.
Constipation	Dandelion, Nettles, Sorrel	All work as a gentle laxative.	Take as tea. Add dandelion leaves to salads. Eat sorrel as a vegetable.
Cough	Garlic, Thyme	Both act as antibacterials, and thyme works as an expectorant.	Use both in food. Thyme may also be taken as a tea, and its essential oil may be used for inhalation.
Cramp	Rosemary, Thyme	Stimulate blood flow and remove lactic acid build-up.	In food, and add to warm baths.

condition	superherb	effect	how to use
Cystitis	Dandelion, Garlic, Juniper berries	Dandelion leaves provide an effective diuretic. Garlic provides antibacterial and antifungal benefits for cystitis often associated with thrush caused by fungal infection. Juniper berries provide specific urinary antiseptic qualities.	Take dandelion leaves as tea as part of high fluid intake and include in salads. Use others in food.
Depression	Basil, Hops, Lemon balm	Basil helps relieve the anxiety that often accompanies depression. Hops are a powerful calmative and improve sleep quality. Lemon balm relaxes physical tension	Add basil to salads and sandwiches. Use hops as tea; also place dried hops in sachets inside a pillow case. Drink 2 or 3 cups of lemon balm tea daily.
Diarrhoea	Garlic, Marshmallow, Mint, Sage	Garlic helps relieve diarrhoea caused by food poisoning. Marshmallow is rich in soothing mucilage. Mint works as an effective antacid and helps to settle the stomach. Sage is astringent and cleansing to the gut.	Use garlic generously in cooking; slice a clove and eat in sandwich at bedtime. Add marshmallow leaves and flowers to salads; also use to infuse oil; make tea from the chopped root. Use mint in cooking; drink as tea after meals. Drink 2 cups of sage tea daily.
Diverticulitis	Marshmallow, Mint, Sage	Marshmallow is rich in soothing mucilage. Mint works as an effective antacid and helps to settle the stomach. Sage is astringent and cleansing to the gut.	Add marshmallow leaves and flowers to salads; also use to infuse oil; make tea from the chopped root. Use mint in cooking; drink as tea after meals. Drink 2 cups of sage tea daily.
Fever	Camomile, Elderflower, Garlic, Marjoram, Onion, Oregano, Sage, Thyme	Camomile is a good anti-fever remedy for children. Elderflower reduces temperatures during the daytime. Garlic is excellent for fevers. Onion reduces temperature. Marjoram, Oregano, Sage, Thyme all have antibacterial and antiviral properties, useful for fever.	Take camomile as weak tea sweetened with honey, 2 or 3 cups during the day, 1 at bedtime. Take elderflower as tea. Crush a garlic clove together with ginger and lemon juice. Bake an onion in its skin for 40 minutes; chop finely; mix in equal parts with honey; take a tsp or 2 every 2 hours. Take the rest singly as teas.

condition	superherb	effect	how to use
Flatulence	Caraway Seeds, Fennel, Lemon Verbena, Mint, Summer Savory	All relieve excessive wind.	Add caraway seeds to all members of the cabbage family during cooking. Take fennel, lemon verbena and mint singly as teas. Add summer savory to bean dishes during cooking.
Fluid retention	Dandelion, Parsley	Both are powerful natural diuretics.	Add dandelion leaves to salads or soups or use to make tea. Add parsley generously to cooking, as a garnish and in salads. Also excellent as a tea; drink 2 or 3 cups daily – but not late at night, as this will disrupt sleep.
Gallstones	Globe artichoke, Horseradish, Tarragon	The globe artichoke is not strictly a herb, but used extensively in herbal medicine to stimulate the functioning of the gall bladder and improve liver function. Horseradish and tarragon are believed to exert beneficial effects on the liver and gall bladder.	Globe artichokes can be obtained as tablets, but better as the whole plant, eaten at the start of a meal. Add horseradish and tarragon to food.
Gastritis	Marshmallow, Mint, Sage	Marshmallow is rich in soothing mucilage. Mint is an effective antacid and helps to settle the stomach. Sage is astringent and cleansing to the gut	Add marshmallow leaves and flowers to salads; also use to infuse oil; tea made from the chopped root is especially good for diarrhoea. Use mint generously in cooking and drink as tea after meals. Drink 2 cups of sage tea daily.
Gingivitis	Oregano, Rocket, Sage, Thyme	Oregano and thyme contain antibacterial essential oils. Rocket is a topical antibacterial. Sage is cleansing and strongly antibacterial.	Use oregano and thyme regularly in cooking. Add rocket generously to salads or just chew a few leaves. Use sage as a hot tea, after every meal and last thing at night.

condition	superherb	effect	how to use
Gout	Dandelion, Lemon balm, Lemon Verbena, Southernwood, Wild strawberries	Dandelion leaves are a powerful diuretic which helps remove uric acid, the cause of the pain of gout. Lemon balm, lemon verbena, and southernwood all have natural anti-inflammatory properties which help relieve the pain. Wild strawberries have specific actions of reducing uric acid levels.	Take dandelion leaves as tea. Use lemon balm, lemon verbena, and southernwood in salads. Eat wild strawberries regularly.
Hair problems	Camomile, Horseradish, Nettles, Purslane, Rosemary	Camomile, nettles and rosemary provide antiseptic qualities. Horseradish improves circulation to the scalp. Purslane contains skin-healing essential fatty acids	Use a warm tea of camomile, nettles and rosemary as an antiseptic final rinse for the treatment of dandruff. Grate horseradish into a sandwich once daily, or take as a tea. Add purslane to salads, especially if dermatitis is present.
Halitosis	Anise, dill or fennel seeds	Freshen breath.	Chew as required.
Hay fever	Elderflower, Marshmallow, Nettles, Thyme	All help relieve symptoms.	A mixture of elderflower, marshmallow and thyme makes an excellent tea for hay fever accompanied by catarrh and blocked sinuses. Also take equal parts of elderflower and nettles as a cup of tea 3 or 4 times a day; start just before hay fever season begins and continue at least 2 months.
Headache	Feverfew, Pennyroyal	Feverfew's anti-inflammatory effects are particularly effective against migraine headaches. Pennyroyal relieves headaches associated with nausea, migraine and travel sickness.	Eat 2 feverfew leaves daily in a sandwich. Take pennyroyal as tea.

condition	superherb	effect	how to use
Heart disease	Dandelion, Garlic, Saffron	Dandelion protects against high blood pressure through its diuretic activities. Garlic lowers blood pressure and cholesterol as well as reducing the stickiness of the blood. Saffron works as an antioxidant and is heart-protective.	Drink at least 1 cup of dandelion-leaf tea daily. Eat at least 1 whole clove of garlic daily in food. Use saffron regularly in cooking.
Heartburn	Mint	The most effective remedy of all: helps relieve heartburn almost instantly.	Take a glass of mint tea sweetened with a little honey after each meal and at bedtime.
Hepatitis	Globe artichoke, Horseradish, Tarragon	Though not strictly a herb, globe artichokes are used extensively in herbal medicine to stimulate the functioning of the gall bladder and improve liver function. Horseradish and tarragon are believed to exert beneficial effects on the liver and gall bladder.	Globe artichokes can be obtained as tablets, but are better eaten as whole plants at the start of a meal. Add horseradish and tarragon to food.
Herpes	Garlic, Lemon balm	Garlic oil is a strong antiviral agent. Lemon balm is specifically antiviral and is a great aid in the treatment of all forms of herpes.	Dab the cut end of a clove of garlic onto affected areas and eat at least 1 whole clove of garlic a day. Add lemon balm to both sweet and savoury dishes, or take as tea; also dab cold tea on any areas affected with the herpes virus, whether it's shingles, cold sores or genital herpes.
Hypertension	Garlic, Juniper berries, Parsley, Welsh onion	Garlic lowers blood pressure and cholesterol, and reduces the stickiness of blood. Juniper berries are a mild diuretic. Parsley helps eliminate excessive fluid, thus lowering blood pressure. Welsh onion has similar properties to garlic.	Eat at least 1 whole garlic clove daily in food. Use juniper berries in cooking. Take a cup of parsley tea 2 or 3 times daily. Use Welsh onion as a garnish on salads.

condition	superherb	effect	how to use
Indigestion	Anise seeds, Camomile, Fennel, Mint	Anise seeds and fennel are excellent remedies for indigestion. Camomile helps relieve abdominal distension. Mint is the most effective remedy of all, relieving indigestion almost instantly.	Use anise seeds and fennel to make tea and drink a cup after each meal. Drink a cup of camomile tea between meals. Take a glass of mint tea sweetened with a little honey after each meal and at bedtime.
Influenza	Elderflower, Ginger, Lavender, Mint, Peppermint, Yarrow	All relieve symptoms. Ginger and mint help soothe irritated tissues.	A tsp of equal amounts of mint and yarrow leaves and elderflowers make 1 cup of tea; sweeten with honey, have 3 or 4 cups daily. A mixture of hot mint and ginger tea with honey is a general all-round soother which also helps fluid intake. Lavender's essential oil dabbed on the temples relieves headache; put into an aromatherapy burner to ease upper respiratory congestion; sprinkle inside the pillowcase to improve sleep.
Insomnia	Hops, Lavender, Scented Geranium	Hops are a powerful calmative which improves sleep quality. Lavender's essential oil is gently hypnotic. Scented geraniums are mildly soporific.	Use lavender in an aromatherapy burner; sprinkle inside the pillowcase to improve sleep. Use hops as tea; place dried hops in sachets inside the pillow case. Take scented geranium-leaf tea with a little honey just before bed.
Laryngitis	Rosemary, Sage	Both help relieve symptoms. Sage eases all forms of sore throat.	Use rosemary tea with added honey as a gargle. Gargle with sage tea.
Menstrual problems	Camomile, Dandelion, Marigold, Nettles, Rosemary, Sorrel	Camomile and marigold ease painful breasts. Dandelion relieves uncomfortable fluid retention before periods. Nettles and sorrel are rich in iron. Rosemary helps relieve painful irregular periods.	Use equal parts of camomile and marigold petals to make tea; apply as a warm compress to each breast for 10 minutes, morning and evening. Drink 2 to 4 cups of dandelion-leaf tea daily. Use sorrel and nettles to make soups. Add strained rosemary tea (4 tsps dried/8 fresh to 600 ml/20 fl oz water) to your bath.

condition	superherb	effect	how to use
Mouth ulcers	Garlic, Lemon balm	Garlic has antiseptic and antiviral properties. Lemon balm has antiviral properties	Rub the ulcers with the cut squeezed end of a clove of garlic; this may be quite uncomfortable, but will heal them quickly. Use lemon balm tea as an antiviral mouthwash.
Raynaud's Syndrome	Basil, Chives, Coriander, Horseradish, Sorrel	All help stimulate circulation.	Add horseradish to appropriate dishes: cold meats and smoked fish. Include others in as many recipes as possible.
Restless legs	Nettles	Rich in iron; restless legs may be an early symptom of iron deficiency anaemia.	Drink at least 4 cups of nettle tea daily; also use as a soup.
Seasonal Affective Disorder (SAD)	Basil, Hops Lemon balm	Basil helps the anxiety that often accompanies SAD. Hops are a powerful calmative. Lemon balm relaxes physical tension.	Add basil to salads and sandwiches. Use hops as tea; also place dried hops in sachets inside the pillow case. Drink 2 or 3 cups of lemon balm tea daily.
Sinusitis	Camomile, Elderflowers, Marshmallow, Nettles, Thyme	Camomile helps clear the sinuses. All help ease symptoms.	Take camomile tea sweetened with honey as a drink; use fresh in a bowl of boiling water as a steam inhalation. Take equal parts of elderflower and nettles as a cup of tea 3 or 4 times a day. Combine elderflower, marshmallow and thyme to make a tea.
Varicose veins	Basil, Chives, Coriander, Sorrel, Yarrow	Basil, chives, coriander and sorrel all help stimulate circulation. Yarrow is rich in bioflavonoids that heal the lining of blood vessels.	Use first 4 herbs regularly in cooking. Take 1 cup of yarrow tea daily; also apply a cold compress of the tea for 10 minutes before bedtime.

sources and further reading

Baker, Jenny. *Cuisine Grandmère*.
London: Faber and Faber, 1994.

Balick, Michael J, and Cox, Paul Alan.
Plants, People and Culture.
New York: American Library, 1996.

Bareham, Lindsey. *Supper Won't Take Long.*
London: Penguin, 1997.

Brownlow, Margaret E. *Herbs and the Fragrant Garden.*
Sevenoaks, Kent: The Herb Farm Ltd, 1957.

Chevallier, Andrew. *The Encyclopedia of Medicinal Plants.* London: Dorling Kindersley, 1996.

Green, Henrietta. *Fresh from the Garden.*
London: Kyle Cathie 1994.

Grieve, Mrs M. *A Modern Herbal*.
Adelaide, Australia Savvas, 1984.

Griggs, Barbara. *New Green Pharmacy*.
London: Vermilion, 1997.

Luard, Elizabeth. *The Flavours of Andalucía.*
London: Collins and Brown, 1991.

MacRae, R, Robinson, R K and Sadler, M J (eds).
Encyclopaedia of Food Science, Food Technology and Nutrition (8 volumes).
London: Academic Press, 1993.

McVicar, Jekka. *Jekka's Complete Herb Book.*
London: Kyle Cathie, 1994.

Nilson, Bee. *Herb Cookery*.
London: Pelham Books, 1974.

Norman, Jill. *The Classic Herb Cookbook.*
London: Dorling Kindersley, 1997.

Page, Mary, and Stearn, William T.
Culinary Herbs: A Wisley Handbook.
London: The Royal Horticultural Society/Cassell and Company Ltd, 1988.

Prince, Thane. *Summer Cook*.
London: Chatto and Windus, 1994.

Rohde, Eleanour Sinclair. *Gardens of Delight*.
London: The Medici Society 1934.

Strickland, Sue. *Planning The Organic Herb Garden.*
Wellingborough: Thorsons Publishing, 1986.

Stuart, Malcolm (Dr). *Encyclopedia of Herbs and Herbalism.* Edgerton International, 1994.

Van Straten, Michael. *The Family Medicine Chest.*
London: Weidenfeld and Nicolson, 1998.

Verge, Roger. *Roger Verge's Vegetables.*
London: Mitchell Beazley, 1994.

Wells, Patricia. *At Home in Provence*.
London: Kyle Cathie, 1997.

Wren, R C (FLS). *Potter's New Cyclopaedia of Botanical Drugs and Preparations.*
Saffron Walden: C W Daniel, 1998.

glossary

Amino acids

Any one of a group of organic compounds that occur naturally in plant and animal tissues and form the basis of proteins.

Anthocyanidin/Anthocyanin

Any of the soluble pigments that produce blue to red colouring in flowers and plants.

Antibiotic

A substance produced by a micro-organism that is able to inhibit or kill another micro-organism.

Antioxidant

A substance that inhibits oxidation. In the body, antioxidants are thought to prevent the destruction of vitamin C, slow the destruction of body cells and strengthen the immune system.

Antiviral

Any substance that effectively fights disease-causing viruses. Garlic and onions have certain antiviral properties.

Beta-carotene

A powerful antioxidant transformed by the body into vitamin A.

Bioflavonoid (also known as vitamin P)

A biologically active flavonoid found in fruits and thought to help prevent cancer.

Capsaicin

A colourless, beneficial irritant found in various peppers, or capsicums.

Carotene

Any of the orange and red pigments that occur in carrots and other plants (as well as in egg yolks and butter), which are converted into vitamin A by the body.

Carotenoid

Any one of the various (usually) yellow to red pigments that are found widely in plants and animals; a beneficial phytochemical.

Chlorophyll

The green colouring matter in plants.

Coumarin

A white substance that beneficially affects blood flow.

Cystitis

Inflammation of the bladder.

Diuretic

Any substance that increases the production of urine by the kidneys. Parsley and dandelion leaves are powerful natural diuretics.

Endorphin

A substance produced naturally in the brain that acts as a natural painkiller and/or tranquillizer. Chocolate is thought to stimulate the production of endorphins.

Enzyme

A chemical substance produced by living cells.

Essential fatty acid

Any of the numerous beneficial fats that occur naturally in fats, waxes and essential oils and are vital for good health. Omega-6 and omega-3 are the two categories.

Expectorant

Any substance that promotes the discharge of mucus from the respiratory tract.

Fenchone

A phytochemical in fennel that stimulates the liver.

Flavonoid

A beneficial phytochemical that tends to occur in plants high in vitamin C.

Folic acid

Vitamin of the B-complex that is used to treat nutritional anaemias.

Free radicals

Naturally occurring oxygen molecules that damage the body and are thought to play a significant role in the aging process.

Gout

Metabolic disease marked by painful inflammation of the joints and an excess amount of uric acid in the blood.

Inulin

A tasteless white substance found mainly in the roots and rhizomes of some plants.

Limonene

A beneficial substance that occurs in the essential oils of many citrus fruits.

Linalool

A beneficial volatile oil.

Lycopene

A carotenoid that forms the colouring matter in tomatoes and is thought to be highly protective against various diseases, including some forms of cancer.

Mono-unsaturated fat

Type of fat believed to offer protection against heart disease and atherosclerosis. Foods rich in mono-unsaturates include avocados, olive oil and peanuts.

Mucous membrane

Any of the membranes rich in mucous glands that line body passages, such as the nose.

Myalgic encephalomyelitis (ME)

A condition that usually follows a viral infection and involves tiredness, muscle pain, lack of concentration, panic attacks, memory loss and depression.

Osteoporosis

A disease involving the weakening of bone that is caused by a loss of calcium.

Organic

Technically, anything relating to or derived from natural organisms, whether of plant or animal origin. For the purposes of this book, the word is synonymous with 'living', 'breathing' and 'natural' – i.e. food that has been grown, cultivated and harvested without the use of harmful agrochemicals or the addition of any chemical additives during production.

Parkinson's Disease

Progressive nervous disease marked by tremor, weakness of resting muscles and a peculiar gait.

Pectin

Soluble fibre that adds bulk and soothes the gut. Apples are particularly rich in pectin.

Phytochemical

Any of the natural chemicals that occur in plants, thought to provide some protection against various degenerative diseases.

Phyto-oestrogen

Any of the oestrogen-like chemicals that occur naturally in plants.

Probiotic bacteria

Beneficial bacteria.

Selenium

An antioxidant mineral that helps protect tissues against damage from free radicals – thus also helps slow the aging process. Brazil nuts are one good source.

Tannin

Any of the soluble, astringent substances found in plants.

Thujone

A volatile oil that is beneficial in small doses.

Toxin

A poisonous substance produced by bacteria.

Uric acid

A crystalline acid that occurs in the urine of most animals. Too much uric acid in the bloodstream can collect in the joints, causing intense pain.

Virus

Any agent that causes an infectious disease. A virus can reproduce only by taking over another living cell.

Volatile oil

An essential oil derived from a plant and bearing its characteristic odour.

Zingiberene

Beneficial volatile oil found in ginger that stimulates circulation.

index